CALLED TO BLESS

CALLED TO BLESS

Finding Hope by Reclaiming Our Spiritual Roots

Robert D. Cornwall

FOREWORD BY
Grace Ji-Sun Kim

CASCADE *Books* • Eugene, Oregon

CALLED TO BLESS
Finding Hope by Reclaiming Our Spiritual Roots

Cascade Books
An Imprint of Wipf and Stock Publishers
199 W. 8th Ave., Suite 3
Eugene, OR 97401

www.wipfandstock.com

PAPERBACK ISBN: 978-1-7252-6868-5
HARDCOVER ISBN: 978-1-7252-6866-1
EBOOK ISBN: 978-1-7252-6867-8

Cataloguing-in-Publication data:

Names: Cornwall, Robert D. | Foreword by Grace Ji-Sun Kim.

Title: Called to bless : finding hope by reclaiming our spiritual roots / Robert D. Cornwall.

Description: Eugene, OR: Cascade Books, 2021 | Includes bibliographical references.

Identifiers: ISBN 978-1-7252-6868-5 (paperback) | ISBN 978-1-7252-6866-1 (hardcover) | ISBN 978-1-7252-6867-8 (ebook)

Subjects: LCSH: Church renewal | Covenants Biblical teaching | Tradition (Theology)

Classification: BL525 .C668 2021 (print) | BL525 (ebook)

This book is dedicated to
Dennis Helsabeck and James Bradley,
who not only taught me history,
but helped me become a historian of and for the church.

Table of Contents

Foreword

ONE OF THE GREATEST concerns for the Christian community today is the increase of young people who leave the church. They leave for different reasons. Many people say that they are "spiritual but not religious" and therefore do not need the Christianity of their youth. However, often, as they leave, their premonitions of some kind of spiritual awakening die. As a result, they continue to fall further from their search for a spirituality that can nourish them and help them through life. They seek other places such as clubs, groups, other religions, friends, etc. for help. Some spiritual searchers can find a sense of spirituality, but others keep searching. However, the hunger for spirituality is not only evident in young people, but prevalent in the lives of those in their middle age and elderly years.

So we ask ourselves, what is spirituality, and why are people seeking it outside the church? Spirituality is the quality of being concerned with the human spirit as opposed to physical things. Spirituality is the long-spanning conduit to come to understand the mystery of God. Spirituality is our lifelong meditation with the divine.

As we seek to develop our senses of spirituality, we encounter the idea of our Creator. Augustine is famous for saying, "If you understand God, then that is not God." We strive to understand God, but in God's infinite nature we are left to accept that our understanding of God is always limited to mystery. We want to understand the mystery of God who created us and called us God's own.

In the desire to become spiritual, we seek the Spirit of God: the Spirit of God that is in all of creation, the Spirit of God that is in the air, the wind, the trees, the birds, the animals, and in each of us; the Spirit of God is the wind, the breath, the energy that comes to us to give us life and renew our life every day. The desire to come to the fullness of God can come to those who remain to be continually challenged, questioned, and spiritually supported—the desire to come to the fullness of God can come to those who still remain in the church.

As we think about an everyday spirituality that nourishes our minds and bodies, we recognize that it is our understanding of God as Spirit that truly helps us gain a fuller understanding of our own spirituality. We come to recognize that in the Spirit, we as humans are all connected through our connection to God.

In this book, Dr. Robert Cornwall generously shares his life journey of seeking the divine, encountering the Spirit, and living into the Spirit. Cornwall explores spirituality with honesty and reflective sensitivity, asking us what it means to not only encounter the Spirit but what it means to live being filled with the Spirit. His words incite a personal path of lived experiences: from being on sabbaticals to engaging in ministry, he provides contextualizing events that give insight into ways we can come closer to understanding and interacting with God. His own life experience, reflection, and sense of spirituality clarify the lens of finding and seeking the Spirit of Pentecost. In turn, we are given the agency to further examine Scripture and church tradition so that we can try to reclaim theological visions for today and build diverse spiritual identities.

In the pursuit of building diverse spiritual identities, we must reconcile with the future. If the future is open and written, where do we find our hope? Robert Cornwall suggests that we look at our spiritual roots to find the spiritual DNA that provides a foundation for our journey forward. It is here that we find our own divine calling, which is rooted in the calling of Abraham and Sarah, who receive the promise that through their descendants, the nations would be blessed.

With the call of Abraham and Sarah as the biblical thread that connects the chapters, Cornwall suggests that our spiritual DNA is made up of the varied experiences we've had in life, including in our religious life. We live in an age when many Christians have experienced several denominational and religious communities. Many people wonder what to do with these experiences. Should we discard them or reclaim them? Should we integrate them into a new identity? Cornwall suggests that we discern ways of reclaiming our varied spiritual experiences, knowing that as people of faith, who we are is rooted in our families, our friendship circles, and in our religious communities. As we take action, we also must know when to have caution, because not everything is worth reclaiming. We take action and attune our intuitions to what requires change and what requires preservation.

What is true for us as individuals is also true of congregations. This is especially true in an age when people tend to move around from tradition to tradition, bringing their own backgrounds and experiences into the mix. Cornwall believes that we will find hope for the future by tapping into these roots. We're not determined by them, but they're present.

In the theological realm, we so often spend our time looking back; looking back in time at a Scripture created so long ago. However, in this book, Cornwall urges us to look to today. This book makes a vital contribution to the conversation by appropriating the idea of intersectional theology, in that what we believe and what we do as people of faith is rooted in our complex and multidimensional identities and biographies. Cornwall notes that he is a white, straight, married, Protestant male, and that though these are elements of his identity, they are not the sole elements. Thus, he invites us to explore our own identities by sharing elements of his diverse religious background. Though his own identity is thoroughly Christian, he has long been involved in interfaith work, a detail that remains present in the book. Thus, over the years he has been Episcopalian, Pentecostal, evangelical (in its broad sense), and is and has been part of the Stone-Campbell Movement. He draws from these richly diverse experiences, values, and characteristics to equip people with the tools to discern their own pathways. These values and characteristics include Tradition, mission, unity, restoration/reset, freedom, and empowerment.

Cornwall approaches this conversation from the perspective of a pastor, trained as a theologian and church historian, and as someone who has a strong background in interfaith work. He uses these angles to weave together a story that invites us to embrace our individual spiritual callings. This book is not only for those in the church, but the young and old spiritual wanderers and inquisitors. I hope that those who have left the church can seek the fortunes immersed in this book for their own spiritual growth. For those who are in the church, this book can renew their visions and hopes for the future. Cornwall's book helps us steer in the right path towards spiritual growth as we unify together in life's journey to find meaning—the endless, and universal quest to discover ourselves, our spirituality, and our God.

Grace Ji-Sun Kim
Professor of Theology
Earlham School of Religion

Acknowledgments

EVERYONE HAS A HISTORY. We all started our lives at a particular moment and place. Along the way, we've added experiences that have contributed to our identities. Whether John Locke is correct in his theory that humans are born as blank slates, our experiences, including spiritual experiences, have contributed to our identities. These experiences can be positive or negative, but we are the product of them (along with genetics, of course). As I wrote this book, the idea of spiritual DNA took hold. In essence, this is a book about discovering our spiritual DNA by examining our faith experiences through the lens of my own faith experiences. Hopefully, the themes you encounter will resonate with you.

In the course of the book, you will come to know me as a follower of Jesus who has a fairly eclectic spiritual identity. Your experiences will be different from mine, but hopefully, the narrative that I try to weave will provide a matrix that will enable you to find hope for the future by taking hold of your own spiritual roots. I invite you to examine not only your spiritual roots, but the roots of our common faith. By tapping into the story of the call of Abraham, I'm inviting you to trace your roots back through Jesus to Abraham. In doing so, my prayer is that you will hear a call to be a blessing to the nations, even as Abraham was given that commission. One important element of this conversation is the recognition that for many of us, our spiritual paths have taken us to diverse spaces. When it comes to congregations, many of them are composed of people whose religious backgrounds are also quite diverse. The day in which the majority of church members grew up in the congregation's denomination is largely over. Hopefully, by reading this book you will find hope and encouragement in the recognition that you're not alone. Part of this recognition involves embracing that diversity of experience as we live our lives before God.

This is in large part my own story, but as with any book, I didn't write it in a vacuum. This book incorporates experiences that I've had as I've journeyed from my original spiritual home in the Episcopal Church to my current home in the Christian Church (Disciples of Christ). Over the past six decades, I have developed an eclectic mix of spiritual homes, to which I will introduce you in the course of the book. The people I've met along the way, starting with my family, have contributed to the story I'm about to tell. Therefore, I am who I am, as a person, as a Christian, as a pastor, as a scholar, and as a writer, because of the many people who have walked this journey with me. This starts with my family members, especially my parents who laid the foundations by taking me to church as a child. Then there are the congregations which I grew up in, was a member of, or have served as a pastor. Each of these congregations has left their mark on me. Then there are my college and seminary professors, especially those professors who were not only my teachers but who contributed to my spiritual formation as a Christian and as a person (I've dedicated this book to two of them). My journey has also been informed by my relationships with peers in the academic world as well as friends and colleagues in the church and interfaith communities. All of these individuals and communities have contributed to the genetic material that makes up my spiritual DNA. This genetic material includes the grace extended to me along the way by God and by those who have accompanied me on the trek.

Having given a general commendation of those who have helped form the context of the book, I need to acknowledge specific people and communities that have contributed to this book, often in ways they may not realize. I begin with the congregation I currently serve as pastor: Central Woodward Christian Church (Disciples of Christ) of Troy, Michigan. The origins of this book are rooted in reflections and research undertaken during my 2013 sabbatical, which the congregation graciously allowed me to take and helped fund. The origins of the chapters that follow can be found in a series of sermons I preached after returning from the sabbatical. These sermons form the core of the chapters. However, I expanded on the messages I shared in those sermons during the sabbatical I took in the fall of 2019. Regarding this sabbatical, I need to thank the Clergy Renewal Program funded by the Lilly Endowment, which gave me the space to gain renewal and take time out to write.

While the ideas that make up the book have their origins in sermons and conversations within the congregation I serve, I was assisted along the way by several people who read various drafts of the book and offered helpful comments and guidance along the way. I would especially like to thank Ray Wheeler, Ron Greene, William Powell Tuck, Jasmine Smart, and Bill Gibson. Their comments and suggestions have made this a much better book. I would like to give special thanks to Bill Gibson, who serves as the director of the Oxford Centre for Methodism and Church History, which provided a research grant that allowed me to spend two weeks in Oxford during my 2013 sabbatical. Some of what you will read has its origins in my time spent in England.

I need to extend my deep gratitude to Grace Ji-Sun Kim, who accepted my invitation to write the foreword to the book. I am grateful for her friendship and encouragement in my own authorial pursuits. As I will note later in the book, Grace's work on intersectionality, a concept I knew little about until recently, has helped me reconceive questions concerning the complexity of our identities, which stands at the heart of the book.

I am exceedingly grateful to Rodney Clapp, my editor at Wipf and Stock, for his guidance in bringing this project to fruition. His willingness to entertain the idea of the book during a conversation at the 2019 AAR/SBL meeting set me on the course to bringing the book to a fitting conclusion. Thanks go to the entire staff at Wipf and Stock for their support of this effort to bring my work to print.

In that regard, I'm pleased that this will be my second book with Wipf and Stock, though this is the first under the Cascade imprint.

Finally, I wish to acknowledge the contribution of my family. Conversations with my son, Brett, who is currently a graduate student in interreligious studies at Claremont School of Theology, have sharpened my understanding of my spiritual identity. My spouse, Cheryl, has been walking with me for the past thirty-seven years as I've walked this path of theological and religious exploration, providing me the room to read and write about subjects that are important to me. Then there is my mother, Beverly Kane, who has given me both support and space to become the person I am today. Because my parents were Episcopalians, I was born into that tradition. My mother made sure I had a good grounding in that tradition. She also put up with my, at times, arrogant declarations of the superiority of a newly embraced faith tradition during my high school years. I can't blame the leaders of the local Foursquare congregation that I joined for my arrogance. That is all on me. Nevertheless, she has always been supportive of me during the many spiritual twists and turns that you will encounter below.

To God, whom I have encountered in Jesus and who has accompanied me through the Spirit who indwells us, I give thanks for that steadfast love that has never left me alone or adrift. It is in this love that I stake my hope for the future of the church and of the world itself.

Introduction—Setting the Course

WHO AM I? WHERE do I come from? Where am I going? What is my purpose in life? These are eternal questions that we all ask of ourselves. Depending on who or what we are, we'll find different ways of answering them. When it comes to defining our identities, we may take into consideration race, ethnicity, culture, gender identity, sexual orientation, family background, and religion. Each of us has a story to tell, which is why genealogical research has become so popular. We want to know who is on our family tree. While our family trees might not include many important figures, most of us have a few ancestors of note. Among mine is John Rogers, the first Protestant martyr to go to the pyre under Queen Mary. What that says about me, I'm not sure, but it is something to take note of. While once upon a time our genealogical research relied mostly on religious and governmental records, along with family stories that have been passed down from one generation to the next, now we have access to genetic reports. Sites such as Ancestry.com and 23andMe can test our DNA for a fee and tell us a bit about our ancestors' identities. At least from the testimonials in the rather ubiquitous television ads, it looks as if most of us have complicated backgrounds. We may discover ancestors that we never expected. We may also discover that some of the stories we've been told about our families are untrue. Oh, and along the way, if we choose this path, we might even discover a few long-lost relatives.

Tracing our ancestry can be mere fun, but it also can lead to a better understanding of who we are and where we came from. What is true of our personal identities is also true of congregations. The religious communities to which we belong (and possibly lead) are made up of people whose backgrounds, while they may seem similar on the surface, can be rather complicated if we dive deeper into each other's stories. While we can't take religious DNA tests, we can tell our stories. We can share with each other about our spiritual journeys, including the traditions we've inhabited. In doing this we'll discover that many of us have traveled through a variety of denominations and even religious traditions. We bring these backgrounds into the congregation, adding to its spiritual DNA. While we might not celebrate everything that is part of our ancestry (there are likely a few skeletons in the closet that we would rather leave there), nevertheless that ancestry—whether familial, national, or religious/spiritual—has helped form us as communities and as persons.

In a sense what follows is an expression of intersectional theology, or at least my appropriation of that emerging expression of theology. Grace Ji-Sun Kim and Susan Shaw, in their introductory textbook on intersectional theology, note that theology is "deeply personal." They write that "each of us has multiple intersecting identities formed in our interactions with other people, social institutions, and systems of oppression."[1] They remind us that our theologies don't "exist separately from the stories of which they are a part." They add that we need all the stories of faith to be expressed, "because each of us is uniquely located in relation to difference, power, hierarchy, and privilege," therefore, "we each have some piece to add to the whole fabric of theology; we each offer something others need to learn, and we need to learn what all others have to offer."[2]

What Kim and Shaw write concerning theology applies, I believe, to our spiritual journeys and to the congregations of which we are a part. The point I wish to draw from this is that our life

1. Kim and Shaw, *Intersectional Theology*, 19.
2. Kim and Shaw, *Intersectional Theology*, 21.

experiences, including our spiritual lives, are complex. Therefore, we would be wise to pay attention to the stories of our spiritual journeys. What you will find as you read the book is my attempt to interpret my testimony in the hope that in the telling and the interpreting of my own story, I can encourage others to tell their stories. I'm especially interested in helping congregations find ways of telling stories of the faith so that in reclaiming founding visions and vocations, congregations can see a fruitful path into the future.

This book has its roots in the three-month sabbatical that I took in the fall of 2013. Because the congregation and I were applying for a grant to support the sabbatical, we needed a theme to guide our application process and the experiences both pastor and congregation would have during the sabbatical. The theme we chose was "Reclaiming a Founding Vision," which was the original title for this book. At the time I took that sabbatical in 2013, I was five years into my ministry at Central Woodward Christian Church in Troy, Michigan. We had been having conversations about our identity as a congregation and what the future held for us from the time I arrived. Even before I was called to serve as their pastor in 2008, the congregation had expressed a desire to become a missional congregation. That conversation led to further conversations about our history and how that history contributed to our identity. You see, the congregation I serve as pastor sits in the suburbs of Detroit, but it was born in the city. Like many predominantly white congregations sitting in major cities with changing demographics, it followed its membership and migrated to the suburbs in the late 1970s. One of the questions that the congregation had wrestled with from the time it moved to Troy was the relationship of where they were now to where they had once been located. So, one of the conversations we had concerned the implications that our prior location had for our current ministry. Being that I am a church historian, this question fits my academic interests, but it also drew on my own spiritual journey, which as you'll see below is rather complicated. In the course of the 2013 sabbatical, therefore, I took the opportunity to explore my own spiritual journey by looking back at the different traditions that contributed to my spiritual DNA. At the same time, this focus allowed the congregation to ponder its own history and the contributors to that history (both past and present).

In the course of my sabbatical experience, I traveled to Oxford, England, where I spent time in the Bodleian Library (University of Oxford), engaging in research on the Nonjurors (an area of scholarly interest). Since I was visiting England for the first time, I took the opportunity to explore what I considered important historical and spiritual sites. I then traveled to California, where I visited the Episcopal church where I had been baptized as an infant, as well as the mother church of the International Church of the Foursquare Gospel (another stop on my spiritual journey). I also paid a visit to the seminary that had formed much of the evangelical part of my identity. Later on, I traveled to Nashville, where I spent time at the Disciples of Christ Historical Society working through the papers of Edgar Dewitt Jones. Jones had served the congregation I now serve from the 1920s through the 1940s. His influence, though more diffuse today as the number of members who had experienced his ministry has been growing increasingly smaller, continues to be felt in the congregation. When I returned from the sabbatical, I gathered with the congregation for a retreat so we could compare notes. I also prepared and preached a series of sermons on the theme "Reclaiming a Founding Vision." At the time I thought these sermons might make for a worthwhile book project, but time intervened and I moved on to other projects.

In the fall of 2019, I embarked on a second sabbatical. During this sabbatical season, I decided to work on one of the writing projects I'd started but hadn't finished. The project that called out to me was the one I had begun six years earlier, the one focused on "Reclaiming a Founding Vision." Seeking a biblical thread to connect the stories, I turned to the call of Abraham in Genesis 12. In calling Abraham, God promised to make his descendants a community of blessing. I hope that those who read to the end will be blessed and, as a result, become a blessing to others.

In rooting the book's message in the call of Abraham, I am very aware of the danger of supersessionism. Therefore, I need to make it clear up front that in appropriating this story I am not suggesting that Christianity supplants or replaces the Jewish people in God's covenant. I affirm the premise that Christianity is rooted in and dependent on Judaism and its origins for our own origins. Jesus and Paul were Jews. They remained Jews their entire lives. I have been blessed by my friendships and ministry partnerships with Jews. I remember well viewing Mel Gibson's *Passion of the Christ* with my friend and partner in writing and in ministry, Rabbi Arthur. As the movie ended and I sat there numb from the overwhelming violence of that film, Arthur turned to me and asked if I was okay. This, after we watched Jews portrayed in horrific ways. Yes, my Jewish friend and colleague was concerned about me. I will never forget that moment as long as I live. In fact, I believe this was a defining moment in my journey.

Christians claim the status of being children of Abraham, but we are not the only children. We don't supplant our older siblings. In fact, we should relish their witness. Our relationship with Abraham is through adoption. As Paul puts it in his Galatian letter, "Just as Abraham 'believed God, and it was reckoned to him as righteousness,' so, you see, those who believe are the descendants of Abraham" (Gal 3:6–7). Therefore, if we hold fast in our belief or trust in Christ, then we can share in the promise given to Abraham, that his descendants would be a blessing to the nations (Gal 3:29).

In the chapters that follow I will weave together elements of my own spiritual journey with the story of my current congregation to provide a narrative that speaks to individuals and congregations who are seeking to discern their own spiritual identities. This book, as conceived, has two audiences. The first audience includes persons like me, who have migrated through a variety of faith traditions and seek ways of integrating those diverse elements into holistic spiritual identities that honor and build upon the complexity and diversity of their experiences.

As readers move through the book, they will encounter a variety of emphases that have helped form my spiritual identity. The hope is that in reflecting on the values and experiences expressed here, readers will be encouraged to explore their own journeys, and then take hold of the covenant promise made to Abraham, that through his descendants, the nations would be blessed (this is a declaration I'll repeat regularly in the course of the book). In sharing these vignettes from my life story, I don't mean to suggest that they are in any way normative or prescriptive. Some elements from my journey might be more helpful than others. At the same time, theology and biography tend to intersect.

Each of us enters the conversation about spiritual identity from a particular context. I happen to be a highly educated, middle-class, white, cisgender, heterosexual, married, male Christian. In other words, I write from a point of privilege. I also recognize that too often persons who share my identity have assumed, as Grace Ji-Sun Kim and Susan Shaw note, that theology has been treated "as something pure, pristine, and nonsyncretistic. Theology has mostly been a monochromatic and one-sided discourse that does not take seriously voices from the Global South or voices of women or voices of other marginalized groups."[3] They have suggested as I've noted earlier that we approach theology from a different perspective, one that gives room for other voices. This book represents my voice, but it is not the only voice that should be heard in the church. So, some who read this book will share my point of departure. Others will not. It's important that we recognize and identify our points of departure, even as we add our own elements to the larger story.

I've written this book with a second audience in mind. This audience is composed of congregations who are also wrestling with the question of identity as they look to the future. They know that change is in their future, but they also want to remain connected to their congregational heritage. The questions for congregations that follow each of the chapters are similar to those I've written for individuals, but they also tend to be more expansive. This is a reminder

3 Kim and Shaw, *Intersectional Theology*, 12–13.

that we do not take our spiritual journeys alone. Even those who claim to be spiritual but not religious tend to look for partners with whom they can compare notes and maybe even undertake their pilgrimages. When it comes to the religious communities in which we find ourselves, the members of these communities likely will encompass diverse spiritual identities. I have taken up that reality in the final chapter of the book, which is based on the final sermon of my sabbatical series. In that sermon and in this chapter, I ask the question: "What is in a name?" I raised this question because the congregation I serve took its name from a specific point of origin in Detroit. Even though the move to Troy took place decades earlier, we've not shed our earlier name. This suggests that continuity of identity still exists, even though we are now a very different church from the one that sat on Woodward Avenue in Detroit. While the congregation may eventually change its name as the number of members who remember the prior location dwindles, the name persists. So, what does that name have to say about the identity of the church in the present moment?

It was in the 1840s that the congregation known today as Central Woodward Christian church began its life in Detroit. Like many congregations, it was born in a home, but over time it grew into one of the largest and most influential congregations in the city and the denomination. Unfortunately, time has not been kind to the congregation (something it shares with many other congregations that were once large and influential). As with many predominantly white mainline Protestant congregations, it thrived in the post–World War II years. Nevertheless, decline set in during the 1960s as Detroit began its own population decline (featuring white flight to the suburbs). The church tried to hang on, but by the mid-1970s it followed the majority of its members into the suburbs.

When I arrived in 2008, the congregation, which had experienced a period of disruption over the previous decade, was in the process of discerning a call to pursue a missional vision. As part of that work, we had conversations about our history and our connection to the congregation's life in Detroit (see chapter 8, "What's in a Name?"). One of the decisions we made after I arrived was to find ways of connecting our ministry in the suburbs with ministry in the city. With that in mind, we helped launch a ministry in the city that continues to thrive called "Rippling Hope." This seemed an appropriate way to reconnect with a founding vision of the pastor who brought together several Detroit congregations in the mid-1920s to form the church that exists today—though it was transplanted to another location. Now, more than a decade later, we continue to discern who we are as a congregation, including what it means to be missional. We have begun conversations about the future, including what we might look like after my eventual retirement. When we near moments of transition, we face the questions of what to take with us on the journey and what to leave behind. This is true of us as individuals and as congregations. It might involve leaving behind a name that has defined us for nearly a century, or perhaps changing the name isn't necessary. Conceivably there is spiritual DNA carried by that name that is worth keeping. Time will tell.

During my fall 2019 sabbatical, which the congregation and I themed "River Crossings," both the congregation and I spent time considering the question of transition and what it might mean for us. Transitions in pastoral leadership can be traumatic or they can lead to new adventures. How we move toward them, through them, and out of them will contribute to the congregation's future. It is good to remember that congregations and individuals have a history and a future, and both influence the present (for good or ill).

As I've noted earlier, one of the questions that will be explored in the coming pages has to do with congregational identity. While this conversation involves examining our past, it also involves how our current makeup influences our journey into a future that remains open and unknown. We have a calling to follow the lead of a God who continually invites followers to move toward unknown lands. We go on this journey as a family that is diverse in its makeup. Even though the congregation I've served remains predominantly white, we bring a diverse set of traditions and identities into the mix. There may have been a time when this congregation's membership was rather stable and most new members were members of the congregation's denomination. In other words, they may have already known the backstory of the church; that's no longer true. We have long-time members who know nothing other than the congregation and its denomination, but most newer members bring to the congregation a different set of stories. So, how might these stories merge into the ongoing story of the congregation?

Something similar might be true for us as individuals. There are those in our midst who were born and bred in the congregation and the denomination. I have clergy friends who can claim several generations of affiliation with the Stone-Campbell/Disciples of Christ tradition. I am not one of them. My own spiritual journey has taken me into a fairly wide assortment of traditions, ranging from Episcopal to Pentecostal. In some ways, the history and core values of the Disciples of Christ denomination fits my personal story, which I will be sharing in more depth as we move forward.

The question I want to raise in this book concerns the nature of our spiritual identities, both as individuals and as congregations. When we think about how our spiritual identities have been formed, how does the past influence the future? Do we embrace the past or do we seek to move beyond it? What I would like to do in this book is share my own story in such a way that individuals or congregations might feel encouraged to explore their own stories as the foundation for looking forward into the future. That process might involve letting go of elements from the past. Or it might involve embracing the past as a foundation for moving into the future. Moving forward may involve grieving losses from our past. We may need to take time to dwell for a moment in nostalgia. In doing so, we can honor the past without getting stuck in it. Michael Girlinghouse contends that nostalgia serves as a coping mechanism that "helps us adapt to the present by drawing strength from past experiences." That is, "nostalgia may refer to the past, but, unlike yearning, it tends to be forward-looking. Nostalgic thinking provides a sense of continuity with the past, linking the past to the present, and opening up possibilities for the future. Unlike yearning, which traps us in the past, nostalgia is a dynamic and motivational force that can help us take proactive action as we step into the future."[4] While I tend not to use the word "nostalgia" in this book, Girlinghouse's definition gets at what I'm trying to do here.

In accepting Girlinghouse's definition, I can admit that there is a bit of nostalgia present in this book. At times I may look back wistfully to elements of my own experiences, while at the same time recognizing that there are elements that I've had to let go of to move forward with my life. I hope that we can uncover hidden treasure in the past that can inform the future, which I believe is open.

As I've looked at my own story, I've discerned principles and values that I think might prove helpful to others due to the course of my journey. These include the value of tradition as well as restoration, mission, and spiritual empowerment, along with freedom and unity. The values I explore are ones that have been part of my own journey. As you read the book you may discover other elements from your journey that can be added to the equation. That is because your journey has taken you to places to which I've not traveled. That is all to the good. In other words, this is a collaborative effort.

In the course of our journeys as individuals and as congregations we gather mementos that remind us of where we've been and that help us conceive of where we might be going as we venture into the future. Because I have adopted a theological perspective that suggests that the future is open, which means God has not predetermined the outcome of history, the choices we make along the way help determine what the future looks like. Nevertheless, even though I embrace an open future, I can also confess with Saint Augustine that our hearts will be restless until they find their rest in God.[5]

---

4. Girlinghouse, *Embracing God's Future*, 39.
5. Augustine, *Confessions*, 3.

First a word about congregations. I believe that congregational identity has roots in the past, including its origin story. We needn't try to preserve or replicate the past in either the present or the future. That would hinder the work of the Spirit of God. Nevertheless, for good or ill, the past does influence the identity of a congregation and the way it lives in the world. It does us no good to ignore the past. In fact, there might be, and probably are, resources from our histories that can help guide the way the church navigates its way into the future. There will also be "stuff" from the past that must be jettisoned. Predominantly white congregations will discover the presence of racism in the past that continues to haunt the present. They likely will find the presence of sexism as well. Nevertheless, they will also find buried treasure that can be brought into the present and can provide a foundation for the future. Discerning what is dross and what is treasure is a difficult but necessary process. This is especially important for congregations, like mine, that have a glorious past that now seems lost.

I realize that conventional wisdom suggests that congregations (and individual believers) should let go of the past so they can move into the future. There is wisdom in this advice because it's easy to get stuck in the past. This is especially true for what were once large and thriving congregations that have experienced significant decline. Many a congregation finds itself living in a building that seats a thousand or more while Sunday attendance runs at one hundred or less. If they are going to experience a positive future, they may need to let go of that building and find quarters that are more suitable for the present situation. That's the practical side, but there is also an eschatological reason for letting go of elements of the past. The Christian faith is oriented toward the future, because like Judaism and Islam it has a linear vision of time and place. Although many Christian communities use a liturgical calendar to guide their worship, moving from Advent to Christ the King Sunday, before starting all over again, each time we run through the cycle we move forward. The eschatological message present in this journey involves judgment, but with a purpose.

That purpose is the reconciliation and healing of all things through Christ (Col 1:19–20).

While the three Abrahamic religions offer a linear view of reality, in that all three assume that God is to be found not in the past but in the present and the future, all three traditions look back to founding principles that are enshrined in sacred texts. So, without giving up that eschatological vision, it behooves us to examine our roots so we can discover what is present in our spiritual DNA. Then we can proceed faithfully into the future, while we remain anchored in those founding visions present in our sacred texts. We might start the conversation by looking at the story of Creation. Or we might want to start with the call of Abraham and Sarah (along with Hagar).

Our task as congregations and as individuals is to find the proper balance between the *alpha* (past) and the *omega* (future) while living fruitfully in the present. Margaret Bendroth puts it this way: "When twenty-first-century Christians gather to sing and pray, when they practice the sacraments of baptism and communion, they are not making up those forms on the spot. All of those are an inheritance from centuries of Christian belief and practice."[6] Yes, some things probably should be tossed, but not everything. There is much to treasure because our spiritual lives are formed by what has transpired before us.

During my 2013 sabbatical and then again during my 2019 sabbatical, I had the opportunity to visit ancient cathedrals and churches that stand as symbols of the church's movement through time. These cathedrals bear witness to the lives of the saints who have gone before us. To give but one example, while visiting the cathedral in Cologne (Köln), Germany, I had the opportunity to view the golden reliquary that is said to contain the bones of the magi. Our guide told us that the decision as to whether the box contains the bones of the magi is a matter of faith. We can test them and perhaps discern their age and origins, but that doesn't prove the truth of the story. While I tend to be skeptical of such things, I confess that I felt something spiritually enlivening by

---

6. Bendroth, *Spiritual Practice of Remembering*, 9.

contemplating these relics housed in a golden box in an ancient cathedral. These might not be the bones of the magi, but their story plays an important role in the gospel message. So, I pondered the story of sages who came from far away to visit the village of Bethlehem so they could honor the Christ child. I thought about how these bones made their way first to Constantinople and then over time found their way to Cologne. In the spirit of the moment, I decided to light a candle and say a prayer as a fellow pilgrim on a faith journey that finds its roots in Bethlehem and even beyond Bethlehem back to Abraham and Sarah, who received a call from God to bid farewell to their homeland and take off for a land they did not know. We are all on journeys, and these journeys help form us. We can ask the "what if" questions, but the choices we didn't make do not define us. That is because I do not know where we would have landed had we not taken the other fork in the road. Each choice is fateful. The truth these cathedrals bear witness to is that we are not the first Christians to follow Jesus, and we will not be the last. Each of us will take different forks in the road, and in making these choices we help determine our future.

As you will see in the chapters that follow, my journey has led me into a wide variety of Christian traditions (all Protestant). Each of these traditions has contributed to my own spiritual DNA. Additionally, over the years I have become actively involved in interfaith work, and that involvement has deepened my spiritual life. I am both more open to other faith traditions, and more rooted in my own. Therefore, I offer the book to individual readers as a word of encouragement and perhaps even guidance as they explore their own spiritual journeys. In other words, I hope my own story can help others integrate their past experiences into a fruitful whole—a sort of mixed-berry pie (here in Michigan, cherries are often added to the blueberries, raspberries, and blackberries, to form a "four-berry pie").

When it comes to congregations, I hope the book will provide a foundation for exploring their own histories and a path toward discovering how the gifts and experiences of past saints and current saints help form the congregation's identity and sense of mission.

We might want to think in terms of how families are formed as two people bring their distinctive histories and DNA into the mix to create the next generation. It may be the historian in me, but I hope that if congregations make use of this book, they can look back at their own histories in ways that inform and empower their future. This isn't about nostalgia. It's about finding our roots so that we can discover who we are in the present and going forward into the future.

There is another way of looking at this journey. We might think in terms of visiting a pawn shop or an antique store and finding hidden treasures mixed in with a lot of junk. If you've ever watched *American Pickers*, you know how this works. There is both treasure and junk in our personal and congregational histories. It takes discernment to decide which is treasure and which is junk. Some things need to be set aside, while other things might be reclaimed and repurposed. When it comes to congregations, I contend that if they can touch base with their founding visions, congregational members can rediscover that first love which led to the founding of that congregation, so they might move forward into the future with confidence.

Returning to the autobiographical part of the book—what you might call my spiritual testimony—each of the chapters that follow touch base with different elements of my faith journey. I realize that many people stay in the same denominational tradition, and perhaps in the same congregation, their entire lives. I know people who can trace back their denominational heritage multiple generations. That can be a real blessing to them and their families. That is not true for growing numbers of people, who may have wandered through several traditions. Sometimes those transitions have been hurtful, and other times they are simply a matter of different needs at different times in one's life. Sometimes there might be a bit of both, which is the case for me.

There may be the need for a person to let go of past experiences so their present and future spiritual experiences can be fruitful and even healing. For others of us, we might feel the need to integrate some of the treasure that we've brought along from our past experiences. That is what I've tried to do in my own life. My spiritual journey led me from the Episcopal Church of my birth through Pentecostalism to my current home in the Christian Church (Disciples of Christ), which is a branch of the Stone-Campbell Movement (often called the Restoration Movement). There have been other contributors to my spiritual makeup that I've experienced along the way, including stops at an Evangelical Covenant congregation, a couple of Baptist churches, and a Presbyterian congregation. If your journey is anything close to my own, perhaps you will find my story encouraging (though others might find it disturbing!).

I want to set this journey we'll be taking within the biblical story. There are several possible starting points, but I decided that the call of Abraham might be the most fruitful starting point. That is because it serves as an origin story for Christians, Jews, and Muslims. Each of these three religions claims Abraham as its ancestor, though we may trace our lineage differently. Nevertheless, that common heritage opens up possibilities for an important interreligious conversation.

The story begins in barrenness. Abram and his wife, Sarai, who was, according to Scripture, barren, had followed Terah, his father, to Haran from Ur. Terah would die in Haran, never making it to the land of Canaan. It was in Haran that Abram received a word from God, calling him to continue a journey that would take them to Canaan. God covenanted with Abram, promising to give his family and descendants the land of Canaan as a homeland so that through them the nations would be blessed. This promise came to Abram, even though he and Sarai had no children and no prospects of having children. Nevertheless, Abram believed God and the rest is "history."

As a Christian, I see this covenant promise fulfilled in the life, death, and resurrection of Jesus. By that, I don't mean that Christianity supplants Judaism as the heir of God's promise made to Abram and Sarai. Again, we must be very careful, as Christians, when engaging with the Jewish foundations of our faith, not to fall into the trap of supersessionism, thinking that Christianity supersedes or replaces the Jewish people as God's covenant people. Instead, I align myself with Paul, who taught that in Christ we who are gentiles have been grafted into the vine that stretches back to Abraham and Sarah, who were promised that their descendants would be a blessing of the nations.

With this biblical story serving as our foundation—our "founding vision"—I invite you, the reader, to discern your own "Founding Vision(s)." While my path might be different from yours, perhaps there is something in my story that can provide a hook for you to hang your own experiences on. In looking at my own path, I've discerned several distinct elements that can be used as hooks. These include continuity (Anglican) and reset (Disciple and Pentecostal), a call to mission (evangelical), and a call to freedom (Disciple and Pentecostal). Along the way, we'll discover that the Spirit of God provides gifts and empowerment (Pentecostal) and a call to unity in diversity (Disciple, Pentecostal, and Anglican). So, let the journey begin.

1

A Founding Vision—A Biblical Story

Go from your country and your kindred and your father's house
to the land that I will show you.... I will bless you, and make your
name great, so that you will be a blessing. —GENESIS 12:1–2

WHEN IT COMES TO tracing our spiritual genealogies, Christians
can consult the genealogies in the Gospels of Matthew and Luke.
Luke traces Jesus' lineage back to Adam, while Matthew traces
Jesus' lineage to Abraham. While we could follow Luke's genealogy back to the creation story, and there is much to commend that
choice, including Paul's declaration that Jesus is the second Adam
(1 Cor 15:45), for our purposes, it seems better to follow Matthew's
genealogy back to Abraham. While Matthew doesn't mention
Sarah, she plays a rather central role in the story, for it is through
her son, Isaac, that Abraham's lineage leads to Jesus (Matt 1:1–16).

While the Christian and Jewish stories trace their origins
back to Abraham through Sarah's son, Isaac, Muslims also claim
Abrahamic lineage. However, they follow a different line of de-
scent, one that flows from Hagar and her son, Ishmael. While the
Genesis account records God's intention for the covenant to flow
through Sarah (Gen 17:15), God made a promise to Hagar as well,
that she would be the mother of a great nation. While it is easy
for us to forget that Hagar and Ishmael were treated poorly by

Abraham and Sarah, God made provision for her and for Ishmael. Hagar responded by naming God as "El-Roi," or "God Sees" (Gen 16:9–16). Debbie Blue calls Hagar "the matriarch on par with the patriarch." She contrasts the decision on Abraham's part to sacrifice Isaac with Hagar's call for God to protect her son. Blue concludes that "Hagar's story isn't grandiose. What makes her inspiring isn't some singular heroic zeal, but something we all have access to in an almost daily way: love." This love is a very human form because it leads her to call out to God to save her child. Thus, Blue writes, "This is Hagar's faith—she sees her child and she longs to satisfy his thirst. She isn't asked to detach from her feeling to prove her faith. Faith is something as close to her, and as natural to her, as her own breath."[1] So, in the end, both Sarah and Hagar will become the mothers of great nations, through whom blessings may flow to the world. As heirs of these two mothers, Christians, Jews, and Muslims have an opportunity to build the necessary bridges that create the possibilities for these blessings to take place.

Matthew's genealogy claims Jesus as both the son of Abraham and the Son of David. Each of these roles is important to the Christian story, but I want to focus on Jesus as the son of Abraham. Father Abraham is the one whom God called to leave Haran and take a journey to a strange land, which leads to the confession that "a wandering Aramean was my father" (Deut 26:5). In taking this journey, together with Sarah, his wife, Abraham embraced the promise that he would become a great nation that would produce blessings for all nations or peoples. As Paul reveals, "Those who believe are the children of Abraham," for "*all the Gentiles will be blessed in you*" (Gal 3:6–9, CEB). That the gentiles (the nations) are to be blessed through Abraham's faith in God's promise is affirmed by the presence of four gentile women in this genealogy. As Eugene Boring and Fred Craddock indicate, "The main reason for Matthew's inclusion of the women corresponds to one of the Gospel's primary themes: the inclusion of the Gentiles in the plan

---

1. Blue, *Consider the Women*, 43–44.

of God from the beginning. The genealogy shows that the Messiah comes from a Jewish line that already included Gentiles."[2]

The message that Matthew and Paul reveal is that in Christ, we who are born outside of Abraham's direct lineage have become his children, and therefore, we are heirs of the promises God made to Abraham and Sarah. Gerald Janzen puts it this way regarding Abraham and the story of redemption: "The biblical story of redemption, as it begins in Abraham, is a journey in blessing from a single person to all the families of the earth. This journey is set in motion by a call from God. For all its brevity, this call is of immeasurable importance, for it both anchors the journey and guides our interpretation of each step along the way—Abraham's, his descendants', and our own steps as we join the journey."[3]

The call of Abraham comes as Abraham and Sarah (then known as Abram and Sarai) are living in Haran. Abraham came to Haran from Ur of the Chaldees with his father, Terah, who was attempting to move to the land of Canaan. Terah would die in Haran, never reaching his appointed goal (Gen 11:27–32). It is in Haran that Yahweh appears to Abraham and directs him to leave behind his current home and head out on a journey to an unknown land (Gen 12). In this first call, Yahweh doesn't reveal to Abraham the destination, which means that if he accepts the call, he will be taking a step of faith. This call comes with a promise that seems impossible to fulfill. God promises Abraham descendants who will form a great nation through whom the nations will be blessed. How might this transpire, considering that Sarah was barren, and the prospects of that changing were dim at best? Nevertheless, this is Abraham's divine commission.

So, how might we, the readers of this story, respond to such a call? The book of Hebrews declares of Abraham and his faith:

> By faith Abraham obeyed when he was called to set out
> for a place that he was to receive as an inheritance; and
> he set out, not knowing where he was going. By faith he
> stayed for a time in the land he had been promised, as

2. Boring and Craddock, *People's New Testament Commentary*, 14.

3. Janzen, *Abraham and All the Families of the Earth*, 15.

in a foreign land, living in tents, as did Isaac and Jacob, who were heirs with him of the same promise. For he looked forward to the city that has foundations, whose architect and builder is God. By faith he received power of procreation, even though he was too old—and Sarah herself was barren—because he considered him faithful who had promised. Therefore from one person, and this one as good as dead, descendants were born, "as many as the stars of heaven and as the innumerable grains of sand by the seashore." (Heb 11:8–12)

Abraham is portrayed in the New Testament as an exemplar of faith, one who responds to God's call despite the evidence at his disposal suggesting that this would be a rather wild goose chase. Such is the journey of faith in a God whose future is open. The way forward requires trust that God will be faithful even as God has been faithful in the past.

We would be wise to stop for a moment and consider the ramifications of taking up God's offer to Abraham. How might we receive it? Families tend to have a strong hold on us and taking off for strange lands isn't necessarily the wisest thing to do, especially if you have a family. It's one thing to head off for Southern California from Oregon in a beat-up Ford Maverick to attend a seminary that had yet to admit you, with no job and no place to live (yes, I did that and was blessed, but I don't recommend it for everyone). It's another thing to take a family on a journey like that.

The call is simple, but fulfillment is not: take your family and head out on a journey that has a destination to be revealed along the way. If you do this, you will become a great nation and through your descendants, the nations (gentiles) will be blessed. They entrust their future to God's call even though the details are sketchy and there is that important caveat—Abraham and Sarah still don't have any children and the prospects of having children are not good. Then again, this is the call of God. As Hemchad Gossai notes, Abraham's calling begins in the context of barrenness (Gen 11:30). Thus, it will take divine initiative for this calling to bear fruit. He writes, "In both Genesis 1 and Genesis 12, God's presence and active generating are essential. In the case of human understanding, beginning from a state of nothingness is out of the realm of reality. However, in Genesis 1 and 12, God employs barrenness, both literally and metaphorically, as a point of beginning."[4]

If this promise is going to bear fruit it requires divine initiative, but also human response. So, how did Abraham know that God would be true to the promises attached to the call? It is worth noting that the original conversation between Abraham and Yahweh is not accompanied by any direct manifestations of divine power, unlike that which came with the Sinai covenant. Bruce Feiler writes that "Abraham, by contrast, witnesses no physical manifestation of God's existence—no burning bush, no dead frogs, no tablets, no water sprouting from a rock. Worse, the voice doesn't even introduce itself. Subsequent biblical figures learn that this disembodied eloquence belongs to the 'God of Abraham' and usually hear a brief curriculum vitae. Abraham receives no such credentials."[5] Abraham follows this voice despite not truly knowing who it is who is calling. This is a call given by an "unprovable god," which according to Feiler, suggests that "Abraham is a visionary."[6]

The journey we are on requires that we, like Abraham and Sarah, take a journey of faith without knowing what lies at the end of the journey. This an open-ended journey, but as the book of Hebrews reminds us, "Faith is the assurance of things hoped for, the conviction of things not seen" (Heb 11:1). Here is where differences in theology might come in. If, like me, you believe the future is open, then taking this journey involves certain risks. The decisions we make along the way have real consequences.

After I graduated from college, I intended to matriculate at a seminary in Tennessee but ended up going to Fuller Theological Seminary in Pasadena. Had I gone the Emmanuel route my entire life would have been different. Perhaps in an alternate universe that path does play out, but to my knowledge that is the realm of science fiction and not modern science. I made a choice and that

4. Gossai, *Barrenness and Blessing*, 5.

5. Feiler, *Abraham*, 40.

6. Feiler, *Abraham*, 41.

choice led me down a particular path that is still in the process of playing out as I make choices that continue to shape my future destiny.

In the case of Abraham and Sarah, if they are to experience the promise that leads to blessing the nations, they'll have to put their trust in this "unprovable god." As the story unfolds in Genesis, we see that they attempted to outsmart God, as in Sarah's decision to offer Hagar as a surrogate to fulfill the promise (Gen 16). It appears that this wasn't in God's plans, but God was able to adjust the plan to include Hagar and her son Ishmael. Things work out for Sarah, as she has a child of her own, Isaac, which results in a name change. Abram becomes Abraham and Sarai becomes Sarah. It will be through their union that the promise of blessing comes to fruition (Gen 17–18).

Abraham might be an exemplar of faithfulness (Heb 11:8–19), but neither he nor Sarah serves as a perfect moral exemplar. However, following the lead of David Gushee and Colin Holtz we might consider them moral leaders. They opine, "Most moral exemplars do not gather mass followings around a transcendent purpose. Moral leaders do. Some moral leaders are also moral exemplars; others, quite frankly, were a bit of a mess."[7] If we read the story of Abraham and Sarah, their lives, at times, were a bit of a mess, but they proved faithful to God's call.

If we step back for a moment to the original call of God, we need to understand that the promise God made to them carried with it significant challenges, because Abraham and Sarah didn't have children of their own and the prospects for having children was increasingly dim due to their advanced ages. Nevertheless, they put their trust in Yahweh, who has, as yet, done nothing remarkable to warrant their trust, and they head out on the road for this unknown land. Over time this faith would be tested, nevertheless, Abraham and Sarah remain faithful (at least for the most part, for at times Abraham and Sarah take things into their own hands, leading to family problems).

---

7. Gushee and Holtz, *Moral Leadership*, 345.

This call given to Abraham and Sarah is foundational to the ongoing story of the Jewish people, and through them, the call is extended to the Christian community, making it a foundational element in the Christian story. It provides the starting point for Islam as well, though there is one important caveat. In Islam, the promise flows through Hagar, not Sarah, making Hagar a mother of the faith. Through Hagar, the promise flowed to Ishmael and his descendants. For Christians, however, the promise flows through Sarah and her son, Isaac, and ultimately through Jesus to his followers. Their faith would be tested, but in the end, despite Sarah's own laughter (Gen 18:10–15), she bore a son and they named him Isaac (Gen 21:1–7).

We will return to the lineage that leads through Isaac, whom Abraham appears willing to sacrifice (Gen 22), but we should not neglect the story of Hagar and her son, Ishmael. Abraham may have cast him out in favor of Isaac, but Hagar receives a promise from God that her son, Ishmael, will also be the fount of a great nation. The story of Hagar and Ishmael, which is marked by Abraham's rejection of them so that Isaac alone would serve as his heir, is problematic. Thankfully, in the text, God takes care of them, providing sustenance for mother and son and promising that her son would also become a great nation (Gen 21:8–21). Even though the Christian story goes back to Abraham through Isaac, it is important that we not forget the legacy of Hagar and her son Ishmael. Rather than pit the two sons against each other, if we are to understand the promise of blessing given to Abraham in the initial call, perhaps both sons can be founts of blessing to the world. If peace and justice and mercy are to be experienced in this world, then Abraham's legacy as it is expressed through both sons is necessary. Bruce Feiler writes of this legacy for the three faiths that trace their origins to Abraham:

> Fourteen hundred years after the rise of Muhammad, two thousand years after the ascent of Christianity, twenty-five hundred years after the origin of Judaism, and *four thousand* years after the birth of Abraham, the three monotheistic religions were inching toward a

posture of open—and *equal*—deliberation. This state of
affairs set up a new question for the faiths to ponder: Can
the children of Abraham actually coexist?[8]

As I will share later in this book, this legacy has proven important
to my own sense of calling to engage in interfaith/interreligious
conversations and friendships, which are, in my mind, expressions
of blessing.

Returning to the lineage that extends forward toward Jesus,
through Sarah, we discover that though there will be many dif-
ficulties along the way, Abraham and Sarah's descendants will be
fruitful, and they will multiply. Isaac and Rebekah have two sons,
one of whom, Jacob, will be the bearer of the promise to the next
generation. Jacob will have sons of his own, and on it goes until
we reach Jesus, who appears in Matthew's genealogy as a son of
Abraham. It is this Jesus whom the angel declares is Emmanuel
(God with us). He is the one, according to the angel who briefed
Joseph on his fiancée's pregnancy, who should be known as Jesus
because he would save his people (Matt 1:21). As I interpret this,
Jesus is the agent through whom "all the families of the earth will
be blessed." Again, in making this judgment, I do not mean to say
that the Jesus movement replaces Judaism. Instead, I am asserting
that through Jesus, gentiles (the nations) are brought under the
covenant promise. That is how, I think, Paul understood his mission as he headed out from Antioch.

In the chapters that lead up to this event in the life of Abraham and Sarah, we see a world fall out of relationship with God,
which leads to confusion and discord. There is the exile from Eden,
the murder of Abel by Cain, the flood, and more. In other words,
humanity, those who were created by God in God's image, get lost,
and can't find their way home. So, how does humanity find its way
back home? How might the divine-human relation be restored?
The biblical story is founded upon a series of covenants, one of
which is made by God with Abraham and Sarah, along with their
descendants, including Jesus (according to Matthew) and those

8. Feiler, *Abraham*, 196.

who have become part of this family tree through faith in Christ (Rom 4).

I appreciate the way John Holbert speaks of the Genesis 12 story. He calls it "the Bible's lynchpin, because the remainder of the biblical story will be one attempt after the other to reconstitute a broken world; God will be persistent and creative with divine ideas that God hopes will lead at last to shalom."[9] From that point on, God works through the descendants of Abraham and Sarah—both biological and spiritual—to bring wholeness to a broken world. This is the blessing that God promises to Abraham and Sarah and to us. It is a blessing that is transmitted to us through the person of Jesus, who is, for Christians, the seed of Abraham. As Paul writes to the Galatians, if in baptism "you belong to Christ, then you are Abraham's offspring, heirs according to the promise" (Gal 3:29). Thus, to be in Christ means that one is a child and heir of Abraham and Sarah and therefore heir to the promise that it is through these descendants that God will bless all the families of the earth.

When I was approached about coming to serve as pastor of Central Woodward Christian Church in 2008, the message that I heard from the search committee and the leadership of the congregation—the message that caught my attention—was that the congregation wanted to become a missional congregation. The interim pastor had introduced them to this concept, and it was taking hold, though not everyone truly understood what that might mean for them. We're still learning about what this means more than a decade later. A few months after my arrival, the congregation gathered for a retreat so we could discern a set of core values that would guide the congregation as we moved forward together. We needed to define what it would mean for us to be a missional congregation. Although we didn't explicitly draw upon the call of Abraham and Sarah during that retreat, it is that call to be a blessing to the nations that defines what it means to be missional. One could say that Abraham's calling served as the first Great Commission, a commission that was reissued in Acts 1 and Matthew 28.

---

9. Holbert, "Lynchpin of the Bible."

The church's calling is an ancient one that is expressed in different ways in different times and contexts, but in all cases, the church is simply fulfilling the call to participate with God in reconstituting a broken world. My own denominational tradition expressed this vision through an identity statement that has called on Disciples churches to be "a movement of wholeness in a fragmented world."[10] This seems to be a rather bold statement, especially for a rather small denomination, but in embracing this identity statement Disciples of Christ churches do not presume to have achieved wholeness. This is simply a recognition that the church is on an eschatological path toward experiencing the fullness of God's realm, a pathway first set forth in the call of Abraham and Sarah.

If, as Disciples theologian Clark Williamson suggests, the "Christian faith is a way of life and blessing," then to choose against "life and blessing," which "belong together," is "to bring curse and death upon ourselves. Curse is what we get when we sinfully reject God's gracious blessing. Blessing is freely offered as a gift, but we have to decide to accept it and allow ourselves to be transformed by it."[11] This is what Abraham and Sarah did. They accepted God's blessing and were transformed by it. Therefore, we can share in their blessedness if we embrace the way of life and way of blessing.

There are a variety of ways of describing this call to share in the ministry of blessing that is traced back to the call of Abraham and Sarah. Some call what we're talking about here wholeness. Others call it reconciliation. According to Paul, God was in Christ reconciling the world to God's self and then commissioning the followers of Jesus to be agents of reconciliation. Still others speak of salvation or shalom/peace. In the Jewish community, this is known as *Tikkun Olam* (to heal the world). These are all descriptions and nuances of that calling to be a blessing to creation so that it might be restored to God's founding vision.

---

10. Watkins, *Whole*, 3–5.

11. Williamson, *Way of Blessing*, 13–14.

Reflection Questions for Individuals

1. Reflect on your own ancestry. Where do you come from? What are your family stories?

2. Spiritually, how do you see yourself fitting into the call of Abraham and Sarah?

3. How might you express this calling in your own life? How might you express this call to be a blessing to the nations?

Reflection Questions for Congregations

1. What is the ancestry of the congregation? What are the congregation's roots—denominationally and more specifically its roots in this place?

2. How does the congregation understand itself as living out the Abrahamic call to be a blessing?

3. What actions might the congregation engage in that would express this sense of being heirs of this promise?

2

Continuity—Tradition as the Interpretation of Founding Visions

You shall love the Lord your God with all your heart, and with all your soul, and with all your might. Keep these words . . . in your heart. Recite them to your children and talk about them when you are at home and when you are away, when you lie down and when you rise. —DEUTERONOMY 6:4–7

GOD CALLED ABRAHAM AND Sarah to go out on the road, not knowing where it would lead. They headed out with only the promise that if they went on this journey the nations would be blessed through their descendants. This serves as a founding story or vision for a people. It is foundational to what is often called "salvation history." While this road to blessing came with a few challenges, mainly because Abraham and Sarah lacked children of their own who could carry on the name, they heard the call and followed this path of blessing. In the end, their prayers were answered, an heir was provided in Isaac, and the rest is "history." So, if we affirm the premise that those who are in Christ are heirs of the promise (Gal 3:29), then the question before us concerns how we embody and share this vision from generation to generation. One way in which this occurs, I will argue, is through Tradition.

It is possible that we can get so caught up in the business of religion that we forget that we are included in this Abrahamic calling. That is, we can get so caught up in servicing the institution, that we forget that we have been commissioned to participate in the work of blessing the nations. Fortunately, God remains faithful to this covenant and has a way of rekindling that vision in our hearts. One way this happens is through Tradition, which passes on the story from one generation to the next. As the writer of Deuteronomy reminds us regarding the commandment to love God with one's entire being (the *Shema*), parents are called upon to "recite them to your children and talk about them when you are at home and when you are away, when you lie down and when you rise. Bind them as a sign on your hand, fix them as an emblem on your forehead, and write them on the doorposts of your house and on your gates" (Deut 6:7–9). Might we call this an act of passing on the "traditions" of the faith?

Protestants tend to resist embracing "Tradition," but if we're honest it's through "Tradition" that the vision of God is passed down through time. Although Tradition is sometimes deemed to be antithetical to the contemporary mission of the church, Tradition isn't the problem. The problem for the church, and individual participants in the Christian community, is "traditionalism." Jaroslav Pelikan has perhaps said it best when he distinguished between these two realities, suggesting that "Tradition is the living faith of the dead, while traditionalism is the dead faith of the living."[1] Therefore, what we need to set aside is traditionalism, not Tradition.

When it comes to traditionalism, tradition (lowercase t) becomes an idol when it is left unexamined and uninterpreted. This occurs when we make the preservation and the repetition of the past an end in itself. Religion becomes nothing but rote actions. It can also come in the form of nostalgia. While nostalgia can be innocuous, it can have a stunting effect on the church. It can keep us focused on trivialities. It often comes equipped with "rose-colored glasses." We envision the past as being simpler—you know, before

1. Pelikan, *Vindication of Tradition*, 65.

technology came to dominate the world (though I can't imagine living without a television set or a cell phone). In general, nostalgia takes us back to a world that never existed, but perhaps we wish had existed. Nevertheless, whether real or not, we can't recreate that world. Besides, truth be told, though my childhood wasn't idyllic, I didn't face the challenges of being African American or Asian or Latino. I might have seen a report here or there on the television news about the civil rights movement or the Vietnam War, but for the most part that wasn't part of my life story.

Nostalgia may have a place in this story, but it doesn't contribute anything of value to our calling as heirs of the covenant made with Abraham and Sarah. When it comes to tradition, it has something to say about the present and the future, but we must beware of making the past an idol. We can't freeze time. Therefore, we can't return to the 1950s when the churches were full and the clergy had an outsized influence in the community. Simply opening the doors of our church buildings won't lead to growth. In fact, we can be actively involved in the community, be respected by members of the community, and not see any growth.

We get in trouble when we pine for a past golden age when the pews were filled and the coffers were overflowing. For many churches (perhaps most), those days have long faded into the past and there is no way to restore this lost glory (if there was truly a golden age). It is appropriate to grieve this loss, but we can't get stuck there.

So why embrace Tradition? Wouldn't we be better off paying attention to the insights of science and technology and business management theory? Though these resources have their place, they aren't sufficient. They don't provide an anchor for the journey forward. Jaroslav Pelikan, who has made a case for Tradition over traditionalism, writes,

> The growth of insight—in science, in the arts, in philosophy and theology—has not come through progressively sloughing off more and more of tradition, as though insight would be purest and deepest when it has finally freed itself of the dead past. It simply has not

worked that way in the history of tradition, and it does not work that way now. By including the dead in the circle of discourse, we enrich the quality of the conversation.[2]

Perhaps it's because I trained as a church historian, but I have found my conversations enriched by including the dead in the circle of discourse. We need not affirm everything that an Augustine or a Calvin or a Wesley taught, said, or did to discover spiritual treasure in their writings and their lives. For example, I don't have to embrace Calvin's vision of double predestination to appreciate his writings about the Eucharist. When it comes to matters of salvation, perhaps Origen and Gregory of Nyssa have words of wisdom that we can learn from. It is true that male leaders and theologians dominated earlier theological conversations, but they are not the only voices to emerge from earlier years. The Tradition of the church incorporates (or should incorporate) the voices of women such as Macrina the Younger (whom Gregory of Nyssa claimed as his teacher), Hildegard of Bingen, Catherine of Siena, Teresa of Avila, Anne Hutchinson, Phoebe Palmer, Georgia Harkness, and Dorothy Day, just to name a few. Even male theologians, such as Augustine, might not be as white and European as we've been led to believe. Justo González has provocatively argued that Augustine was mestizo, in that he was the child of a Roman father and a Berber mother. Thus, his is a mestizo theology.[3] Let us not forget the many untold stories of those who faithfully lived out the Christian faith and passed on their values to the next generation.[4]

How then does Tradition work? As I have come to understand Tradition, it involves passing down through time the story of human encounters with the living God and through the ongoing interpretation and application of the Christian story through time. This is not accomplished by passing down video recordings (which are usually edited, and thus involving interpretation). The basic story line comes to us in Scripture, but over time other stories are added. The same is true for Islam, in that the Qur'an is the sacred

2. Pelikan, *Vindication of Tradition*, 81.

3. González, *Mestizo Augustine*, 14–19.

4. On this see Bass, *People's History of Christianity*.

text, but the Hadith, the traditions and sayings of Muhammad, along with the commentaries on the Qur'an, provide guidance for the Muslim community.[5]

In the Christian context, Tradition can include both oral and written sources. It comes to us through liturgy and sacraments, through art, and even through stone. Consider the stories enshrined in religious architecture. What messages do these buildings share with us? Whether the building is a village church that dates back to Anglo Saxon days or a majestic medieval cathedral, such as the Gothic cathedral in Cologne or the Romanesque cathedral in Speyer, both of which I visited during my sabbatical, these buildings have stories to tell. They carry stories in their crypts and their windows. So, what is it that we hear when we enter these buildings? What do they say about the people who built them and worshiped in them? What do they communicate about the Christian message?

If we return to the origins of our story in the call of Abraham and Sarah, then Tradition offers a living witness to God's covenant of blessing as it has been carried forward through time. If we take Matthew's genealogy as our guide, then this Tradition of blessing starts with Abraham (along with Sarah, who remains unnamed despite the importance of her contribution to this story). It is renewed in the life, death, and resurrection of Jesus. Then, the story gets passed on through time by a church that is born on the day of Pentecost (Acts 2). Over time, this covenant of blessing has been received and interpreted and restated in new contexts from Europe to Africa to Asia to the Americas. Finally, it has been passed on to us. In other words, Tradition is the basic story of faith that has been embodied and expressed in different ways, reinterpreted in each new age, giving meaning to the present.

Although written for another purpose (reflecting on the role of memory in the process of aging), these words of Frank Cunningham seem appropriate here: "Our story is not just a fact-based recall of events, accomplishments, failures, growth, or diminishment. It is also about recognizing an arc of nourishment, a leading

---

5. Mattson, "How to Read the Quran," 1594–95.

theme that fed the multiple phases of our past, a story line that fostered our growth and now helps understand who we are."[6] What Cunningham says about the human aging process can be applied both on a large scale to the story of faith extending from Abraham and Sarah toward a future that has yet to be written, as well as to our own lives. I am a product of my history. I'm not a slave to it, but all that I have experienced in my faith journey informs who I am and how I understand myself in the broad scheme of God's realm.

During my sabbatical in the fall of 2013, I attempted to touch base with some of the traditions that have influenced my own spiritual development. The first stop on my sabbatical adventure took me to England, which reflected both my scholarly interests and my spiritual roots in the Anglican Tradition. The scholarly part of my identity was fed by hours spent with the papers of Thomas Brett, a Nonjuror bishop, who turned to Tradition to define his vision of the church and its sacraments. I'm not sure I am in full agreement, but Brett might have a point when he suggests that God "has appointed *Tradition* as the best and safest guide to direct us how to understand the Scriptures, even in matters necessary to the salvation of all."[7] What I take from Brett's statement is a warning against being too quick in our interpretations, suggesting that we should wait until we've heard from those who have traversed this path before we undertook it. We might learn something valuable in doing so.

Written works from the past bear witness to the story of God's redeeming presence in the world, but there are other forms of witness. Returning to the message written in stone, as noted above among the highlights of my two sabbatical visits to Europe (England in 2013 and the Continent in 2019), I had the opportunity to visit ancient churches and cathedrals. They served as pilgrimage points and not just tourist stops. When I visited England in 2013, I stepped back in time and experienced the rich heritage that is encased in stone and liturgy. Some of the churches I visited go back more than a thousand years to Anglo-Saxon days. One of

---

6. Cunningham, *Vesper Time*, 1.

7. Brett, *Tradition*, 32.

the things you notice as you walk through these churches is the monuments to people long since deceased. These monuments have a story to tell. At Christ Church Cathedral in Oxford, for instance, I found the marker for the burial site of the philosopher John Locke, whose influence has been deeply felt in my current faith community. There is also a marker reminding us that John and Charles Wesley were ordained to ministry in this church. As I contemplated the monuments and the shrines, I felt the presence of the great company of saints joining with me as I joined the congregation in the worship of God. When I went to the altar to receive communion in Oxford and then at St. Paul's, London, I took a journey that thousands of others have taken down through the centuries. Amid these experiences, I felt my "inner Anglican" emerging.

I speak of my "inner Anglican" emerging because my earliest formation as a Christian came in the Episcopal Church. Not long after I was born, I was baptized at St. Luke's of the Mountains Episcopal Church in La Crescenta, California. We moved from La Crescenta before my first birthday, so until a visit in October 2013, I had no visual memory of that church. However, other Episcopal churches helped form me, with St. Barnabas of Dunsmuir, California (now located in Mount Shasta), a congregation in which I got my first taste of service in the church as an acolyte at the age of nine. From St. Barnabas we moved to St. Paul's in Klamath Falls, Oregon. During my years as part of St. Paul's I again served as an acolyte and then as a lay reader and choir member. I may have left the Episcopal Church in my teen years, but seeds were planted, which have contributed to my more mature spiritual identity. Among the seeds planted during this period was an appreciation for Tradition, though I didn't know it at the time. Even though I am part of a non-creedal community I have come to value the witness of these forms of Tradition, including the creeds, even if I do not believe they ought to be used as tests of fellowship.

I appreciate my origins in the Anglican Communion, because of its witness to the value of continuity. The Anglican tradition has historically attempted to balance (not always successfully) both

Reformed and Catholic impulses, and in doing so it has continued to bear witness to the importance of the past. Although Scripture is given first place in the triumvirate of authorities by the Anglican community, Reason and Tradition are recognized as offering Christians important sources of wisdom and guidance in matters of faith and practice. Within the Anglican Communion, the aforementioned Nonjurors of the eighteenth century, especially the Usages Party, which has been the focal point of my scholarly work, made Tradition a crucial component of their vision of the church. In fact, they were intent on restoring the liturgical and sacramental practices of the ancient church and sought to engage the Orthodox churches of the East in reunion conversations. This didn't prove successful once the Eastern churches realized that the Nonjurors were simply a conservative rump of the Church of England (and thus not major players). Nevertheless, the Nonjurors kept Tradition alive in an Age of Enlightenment.

One contributor to the Nonjuror embrace of Tradition was the witness of a fifth-century monk named Vincent of Lérins. Vincent offered a formula for determining what traditions should be welcomed as authoritative: "Moreover, in the Catholic Church itself, all possible care must be taken, that we hold that faith which has been believed everywhere, always, by all."[8] It's possible to take Vincent's canon too far, as some Nonjurors were known to do, but the principle is a good reminder that as important as Scripture is in providing us the primal authority for faith and practice, it still must be interpreted. If we follow Vincent's lead, consensus rather than novelty should be our guide. Not everyone would agree. There always have been alternative witnesses that offered a more "revolutionary" vision of history. But, for the moment, I'll follow Vincent and envision Tradition as the living witness of the church as it bears witness to the continuity of the gospel message and Christian mission down through the ages. This doesn't mean that Tradition has always got it right, because it hasn't. The subtitle of Diana Butler Bass's *A People's History of Christianity* suggests

---

8. Vincent of Lérins, *Commonitory*, 2:6. On Vincent see Guarino, *Vincent of Lérins*. On the Nonjurors see Cornwall, *Visible and Apostolic*, 50–54.

a counterpoint to Tradition by pointing us to "The Other Side of the Story." There is room for consensus (Vincentian Canon) and novelty (the ongoing work of the "unfettered Spirit").[9]

What Tradition does is remind us that while there is always room for new discoveries and new interpretations, not everything that is modern is correct. Simply embracing novelty doesn't lead to greater spiritual awareness. So, when it comes to Tradition, we might want to think in terms of what Keith Stanglin calls "retrieval theology." This involves "not simply replicating or repristinating older theology, but taking the best of theology and, in this case, the best of biblical interpretation from the past and allowing it to inform our own theology and biblical interpretation today."[10]

One place where Tradition bears witness to the continuity of the faith is the Lord's Supper, or Holy Communion. When we gather at the Lord's Table, we do so in remembrance of Jesus, who promised to be with us always. This call to remember is inscribed on my congregation's communion table: "In Remembrance of Me." As we take bread and cup, we are invited to remember that God is revealed to us in the life, death, and resurrection of Jesus. This service of the table isn't a funeral. The one we come to remember isn't dead. Instead, Jesus seeks to meet us at the table so that we might be nourished and fed for the journey ahead, a journey that brings blessings to the nations.[11]

When we read Deuteronomy 6, we hear a call to the people of Israel to remember and pass on their primal story. It is here, in this passage that we hear the *Shema* pronounced, which serves as the Jewish confession of faith, a confession that every Jew must take to heart. There is but one God, and you shall love God "with all your heart, and with all your soul, and with all your might." The people of God are directed to not only remember this confession of faith, but they're called upon to pass this confession of faith on from generation to generation. The people of Israel are told to "recite

---

9. On the freedom of the Spirit, see Cornwall, *Unfettered Spirit*.

10. Stanglin, *Letter and Spirit*, 11.

11. Cornwall, *Eucharist*.

them to your children and talk about them when you are at home and when you are away, when you lie down and when you rise."

Might this suggest that it isn't enough for us to send the children off to Sunday school and hope that this brief experience will suffice? Or might this suggest that we would be wise to make these commands the centerpiece of family life? Parents and those responsible for the lives of children are called upon to help their children incorporate this faith tradition into their own lives so that they too might come to know the living God.

There is a rather constant refrain that I hear in my own denominational circles (I'm a Disciples of Christ pastor), as well as among many other progressive/liberal Christians. That refrain suggests that beliefs don't matter. To be more precise, the issue is doctrine. My experience, however, suggests that what we believe (doctrine) and confess does matter. Beliefs matter because they express our core values. They reflect what we hold to be true about God, the world, and even ourselves. These beliefs and core values are reflected in the way we live in the world. As Christians, our beliefs express the nature of our trust in God.

When it comes to interfaith conversations and partnerships, something that is important to me, what we believe serves as a point of departure for our conversations. My Muslim, Jewish, and Hindu friends (with whom I gather with some regularity for conversation) want to know what Jesus means to me, and I want to know what their beliefs mean to them. You needn't force your faith on your children to let them know what you believe and why. That's the important piece, letting them know why you believe what you believe. They may, in return, teach you something important.

Unfortunately, many Baby Boomers (my generation) didn't heed the words of Deuteronomy. When it came to matters of faith, many parents decided to let their children "decide for themselves." In other words, they didn't make any effort to recite these commands to their children. As a result, many younger adults have had little exposure to the Tradition that has been passed down from generation to generation. So, it's no wonder that the fastest-growing religious group in America is one that chooses not to state a preference. Now I'm not encouraging coercive parenting, but it is important to share that which is most dear to our lives with our children. If your faith is important to you, then share it. It's important to remember that if you don't share what you believe, our children still hear things. What they hear may be that your faith isn't really all that important. They may also hear a problematic Tradition. In the end, they'll need to decide what to do with what has been shared. They may even decide to step away from the faith, and then later reengage because you shared your faith but then gave them space to determine their own path.

The good news in all of this is that God is faithful. There is a Tradition that continues to be passed on from generation to generation, even if it is being left to a remnant. That's okay because that remnant has the opportunity to reclaim the founding vision, which I believe is that we as children of Abraham and Sarah are called to be a blessing to the nations.

Our era in history isn't as unique as we might think. We can look back to that period in European history as antiquity gave way to the medieval era when literacy began to fade among the populace. The monks kept busy copying ancient manuscripts, including biblical texts, so that later generations might have access to these riches. Not only did the monks copy the ancient manuscripts, but the message was enshrined in stone and ritual and stories. The latter is the work of the hagiographers, who told and retold stories about the faithful. We are the inheritors of these traditions. The traditions that are passed down through time needn't become idols. Instead, they can be and are witnesses to the ongoing presence of God in our midst. And as Paul puts it in 2 Thessalonians, "For this purpose he called you through our proclamation of the good news, so that you may obtain the glory of our Lord Jesus Christ. So then, brothers and sisters, stand firm and hold fast to the *traditions* that you were taught by us, either by word of mouth or by our letter" (2 Thess 2:14–15). Or perhaps Ruth Duck is correct in saying that tradition "is not an unchanging heritage but a never-ending process of passing on faith in ever-changing ways."[12]

12. Duck, *Worship*, 265.

How do we keep a forward-looking missional focus while at the same time keeping in touch with founding visions? How do we pass on life-giving traditions without falling into the trap of nostalgia and traditionalism? We do not have to recreate the life that Abraham and Sarah lived, but we can take hold of the vision given to them and then passed on through the centuries until reaffirmed and expanded by Jesus. From Jesus, the vision has continued to be passed on through the centuries until it reaches us. There is a myth that is prominent among some in the Protestant community that God lacked a faithful witness from the end of the first century until their "founder" came on the scene. Thus, it might be the Reformers of the sixteenth century or in the case of my own tradition, the reformers of the nineteenth century. This myth, which continues to be restated, robs the church of its heritage and many riches. As my son pointed out to me, many Christians look East for spiritual treasure, while ignoring the treasures that are present within our own traditions. Consider, for instance, mystics such as Hildegard of Bingen or Teresa of Avila. It's not wrong to look outside the Tradition, but we may be missing something from our own history. Both my son, Brett, and I have found resources within the Orthodox Tradition that speak to us in new ways. I had read and studied Origen and the Cappadocians before these conversations, but now I find in them new sources of insight as to God's expansive love that I may have missed in earlier reads.

The word from Deuteronomy is this: "Keep these words that I am commanding you today in your heart. Recite them to your children and talk about them when you are at home and when you are away, when you lie down and when you rise. Bind them as a sign on your hand, fix them as an emblem on your forehead, and write them on the doorposts of your house and on your gates" (Deut 6:6–9). There is a word to be shared from generation to generation that leads to blessings to all who hear it. It simply needs to be shared and reshared.

Reflection Questions for Individuals

1. What stories have you heard or told about your family history? What do these stories involve? How do they inform your sense of identity?

2. What are the religious/spiritual traditions that have informed your life? What have you gleaned from the history of the church at large? From your denomination? Your congregation?

3. How do you pass on your religious/spiritual beliefs and practices from one generation to the next?

Reflection Questions for Congregations

1. In an age that is future-oriented, what role does the past play in a congregation's life? What does it say about how it navigates the present and prepares for the future?

2. Tradition is a dirty word in some Christian circles, but if Tradition "is the living faith of the dead," what are the traditions of the church that inform its identity? How has this living faith been heard and incorporated into the life of the church without it becoming traditionalism?

3. What steps has the congregation taken to tell the story of the faith, the Tradition that informs the Christian faith? How does this process help the congregation discern its own sense of identity, purpose, and mission?

4. How does this Tradition, including Scripture, get passed on from generation to generation, as Deuteronomy 6 directs?

3

Reset—Returning to the Founding Vision

I also know that you are enduring patiently and bearing up for the
sake of my name, and that you have not grown weary. But I have
this against you, that you have abandoned the love you had at first.
Remember then from what you have fallen; repent, and do the works
you did at first. —REVELATION 2:3–5

TWENTY-FIRST-CENTURY CHRISTIANS, WHATEVER THEIR denomination, are inheritors of traditions. Over time these traditions
have been reinterpreted, adapted, expanded, and amended. At
times these adaptions and emendations have served to preserve
the core message of the faith, but at other times they have obscured
the core message. The word of the angel to the church in Ephesus
commends the congregation for its endurance and faithfulness,
but the angel chides them because they "let go of the love you had
at first" (Rev 2:4, CEB). In other words, despite their faithfulness,
something was amiss in Ephesus, and it was time to reset things.

If we affirm the premise that God's covenant with Abraham
and Sarah is foundational to the Christian mission of blessing
that is embodied and defined by Jesus and then passed on to his
followers, so that gentiles might be brought into the family, we
might wonder how we can stay true to this calling. This covenant
made first in the call of Genesis 12 serves as a mission statement

for the Jewish people, and this to be a blessing to all. Rabbi Barry Schwartz writes that "Abraham's faith will serve as a model for his heirs, through their misfortunes; when they obey; when they stray; and when they wrestle with the covenant stipulations." That is the foundation: Abraham is the model of faithfulness to the covenant. But that is not all; Schwartz continues, "The prophets will uphold the covenant as the measuring stick of our standing before God and each other."[1] That covenant of blessing is the measuring stick by which we judge our adherence to the calling. The role the prophets played in the biblical story is to call the people back when they strayed from the covenant. As we have discerned, in Christ we are drawn into this stream of descendants. Like our predecessors in the Hebrew Bible, we can get off course. When this happens, the Spirit of God finds ways of letting us know that it is time to reset things. History is filled with examples of renewal and reforming movements that seek to return to the founding visions.

As I read Revelation 2, I am reminded that time tends to obscure callings. We may remain faithful and yet lose our first love. We can become overly comfortable with life and then become complacent. It happens in marriage and other relationships. It occurs in churches as well. So, the invitation is given to us that we might return to that first love, as we see with the prophets of ancient Israel who continually called the people back to the covenant that God made with the people in Sinai. This covenant was essentially a reinterpretation and adaption of the earlier covenant made with Abraham and Sarah, though with a narrower focus. The angel takes up this prophetic duty in Revelation 2 by inviting the Ephesian church to "remember then from what you have fallen; repent, and do the works you did at first" (Rev 2:5). To use a computer analogy, whenever the system gets overly corrupted, you have to restore the system to its original factory settings. So it is with the church—whenever we forget who we are and what we're called to do, then it's time to hit the restore button.

If this computer analogy doesn't work for you, then picture in your mind the walls of an old church building that were once

---

1. Schwartz, *Path of the Prophets*, xxxiv.

covered with vibrant colors and designs. Over time the congregation decides that things need to be modernized so they paint over the designs with a rather dull coat of paint. Then one day, when the church building is being remodeled, the restorers peel back the faded and dirty paint and discover that underneath this dullish paint job is the long-forgotten original design. Often what lies underneath is a fresco or mural that reveals the original vision of the congregation. When the church makes this discovery, it may decide to restore the building to its original glory. Often what they find is rather surprising—like evidence of women in leadership in the early church.

A close look at Christian history will reveal many examples of reform movements that emerged in a moment of crisis or transition and called the church back to its original vision. The Franciscan Order was one of those restorationist movements. Saint Francis saw corruption in the church and called for a return to the simplicity of the founding message of Jesus. The reforming movements of the sixteenth century, including those initiated by Martin Luther and Ulrich Zwingli, offer other examples. Still another such movement is the Stone-Campbell Movement that emerged in the early years of the nineteenth century. The challenge for reforming and restoring movements is that they too can forget their original purpose and need their own reset. Indeed, that is the message of the Latin phrase *semper reformata*—always reforming. When we go about reforming something, we need something to serve as the anchor, as the starting point. That is the founding vision. For most such movements in Christian history that starting point is the New Testament. Quite often the anchoring point is found in the book of Acts, specifically the Pentecost story (though nineteenth-century Stone-Campbell restorationists took something different from Acts than did Pentecostals at the turn of the twentieth century).

In the early nineteenth century two recent immigrants to America, Thomas and Alexander Campbell, a father and a son who were ministers in the Scottish Presbyterian tradition, concluded that the church of their day had strayed too far from Jesus' original vision. They also felt a call to restore the church to what they called the "ancient order of things." By that, they meant the church order and purpose they discerned to be present in the New Testament. So, they began their work of peeling away the accumulated "stuff" that now obscured the church's sense of purpose.

It seems that movements emerge regularly seeking to reset things. If the Stone-Campbell Movement represents a nineteenth-century attempt, Pentecostalism represents a twentieth-century restoration movement. The Pentecostal movement continues to grow and make its presence felt on the contemporary church of the twenty-first century, especially in the global south. While there is a distinct Pentecostal movement that emerged from Azusa Street and other early twentieth-century revivals, it has left its mark on a broad sweep of the Christian community, including Mainline Protestants, Evangelicalism, and the Roman Catholic Church.

Like the Disciples of the early nineteenth century, Pentecostals look to the book of Acts for guidance. When they read the book of Acts, they see a people empowered by the Holy Spirit who do miraculous works. Early Pentecostal leaders decided that the modern church needed to be spiritually restored. The means to that end, as they read the book of Acts, involved the restoration of the miraculous dimensions they saw present in the life of the early church. It wasn't enough to restore the church order found in the book of Acts (the intent of the Stone-Campbell restorers). If the church was going to be faithful to the calling of Christ, and bless the nations, it would need the kind of spiritual power evidenced in the ministry of Jesus and by the apostles. Pentecostal theologian Amos Yong writes that "the church is an organic, dynamic, and eschatological people of God called after the name of Jesus and constituted in the fellowship of the Holy Spirit."[2]

I am an ordained minister in one branch of the Stone-Campbell Movement, which tends to have a more reserved view of the Holy Spirit than is found in Pentecostalism. However, before I became part of my current denominational home, I spent several years within Pentecostalism. It was during my high school years, at a time when I was asking questions about the meaning of my

2. Yong, *Discerning the Spirit(s)*, 122.

life and about my faith, that I began to participate first in a Bible study and then moved from the Episcopal church to the congregation that sponsored the Bible study. This congregation was related to the denomination founded by Pentecostal evangelist Aimee Semple McPherson (the International Church of the Foursquare Gospel). I have made several pilgrimages to Angelus Temple, the church that McPherson built in Los Angeles in the 1920s. In fact, I'm probably one of the few Disciples pastors to bring her name and legacy up in sermons. Tracking back to the origins of a congregation or movement is not an act of nostalgia. It is an opportunity to return to first loves, so we might catch a vision for the future.

Sister Aimee (as Aimee Semple McPherson preferred to be known) outlined her restorationist vision in a famous sermon titled "Lost and Restored," which she based on her reading of Joel 2. In this sermon Sister Aimee suggested that as the church moved forward in history it lost something. She suggested that by the second generation the Jesus movement began to lose its moral and spiritual power. This included the loss of the miraculous. Step by step the church lost its vision until things began to turn around with the Reformation. Starting with Martin Luther's efforts, movements emerged that began to slowly restore the church to its original vision. In her vision, Luther restored an emphasis on justification by faith while John Wesley restored sanctification to the church. Then at the beginning of the twentieth century, a new movement of the Spirit broke out at the Azusa Street Revival. In this new movement of the Spirit, God restored the miraculous power of the Spirit to the church. Her vision was one that was shared by many of her fellow Pentecostals. Still, even if what had been lost through the centuries had been restored, the church hadn't yet reached perfection. So, she declared,

> Do not stop short of God's best. If you lay down your crown, another will take it up, the number will be complete, none will be missing, only those who have pressed on all the way to his standard will be caught up. If you have been doubting God, doubt no longer. He is waiting to restore all the years that have been eaten, and cause

you to stand forth in that glorious perfect tree company,
ready and waiting for Jesus.[3]

In many ways, Sister Aimee's theology is different from my own,
but her restorationist vision reminds us that God's Spirit does
move in the church, resetting and restoring things to their original
settings.

This restorationist vision can, like traditionalism, fall into
the trap of nostalgia. That is, we can become satisfied simply with
the idea of restoring what was without any vision for the present
and future. The Campbells and Barton Stone in the nineteenth
century, along with Sister Aimee in the twentieth, understood that
the work of restoration needs to move us into the future so we can
experience full communion with the living God. In other words,
they had an eschatological vision of the work of God in the world
with the goal being the perfection of creation. This move into
God's perfection brings us into full participation in the blessings
of God that mark the realm of God.

In Revelation 2, the Son of Man stands amid the seven lamp-
stands, representing the seven churches of Asia. He speaks this
word of hope to the angel assigned to the church in Ephesus: "To
everyone who conquers, I will give permission to eat from the tree
of life that is in the paradise of God" (Rev 2:7). That is, if we hold
firm to God's calling, we will eat of the Tree of Life standing in
the center of the garden. Although the Son of Man commends the
Ephesians for their hard work, he also brings a word of warning.
Yes, these are good, hardworking people who resist evil and don't
even get weary from their work. While this is a faithful community, something important seems to be missing. Therefore, they
are in danger of having the light of the Spirit removed from their
lampstand. What is missing is their first love.

Yes, they "abandoned the love [they] had at first." We're not
told how this happened, but they're told to repent and return to
the works of love that originally marked the community. In other

---

3. McPherson, *Foursquare Gospel*, 38. See Cornwall, "Primitivism."

words, the Son of Man was telling the angel of this church to press the reset button.

We might not have the details, but I think anyone who has been in a long-term relationship knows that the initial ardor of love can diminish over time. When you're in the early stages of your relationship you bring gifts to each other and spend as much time as you can with each other. Then, as time passes, you might begin to take your partner for granted. You do the expected. You might send flowers on a special occasion like an anniversary, but rarely if ever do you send flowers just because you want to say I love you. Cheryl might remember a young man showing up on her doorstep, bearing a flower—most likely a carnation because a rose was too expensive for a poor seminarian—even though this young man should have been studying for his finals. Yes, first love will do that kind of thing to you. Over time couples tend to become comfortable with each other. They forget that first spark of love. A time comes when it needs to be rekindled—or perhaps restored.

Although the Ephesian church seemed to be doing the right things, the love that they had been known for in the beginning was now missing. In the beginning, their faith was expressed in love for God and their neighbor. But now, it seems to have disappeared. Other things began to crowd their way into their daily lives, so they had lost their focus. They had forgotten the truth that Paul had shared with the Corinthian church—that is, without love we gain nothing. Only love endures, and therefore it is the better way (1 Cor 13). Despite all their hard work and their attempts to be faithful, they had missed the point of their calling. They were religious, but not spiritual. To put it a bit differently, in her book on worship, Ruth Duck writes, "God alone is holy and worthy of our glory and praise. All the good things that can come of worship—education, church growth, cultural relevance, social change—seem to disappear the moment they become the primary goal, though each may be an outcome of worship truly done."[4]

By resetting or restoring the church to its founding vision, we turn our focus back to the God who first loved us, so that we might

4. Duck, *Worship*, 266.

love one another. In this, the nations receive their blessing, which is to taste the fruit of the Tree of Life.

Reflection Questions for Individuals

1. The word in Revelation 2 to the Ephesian congregation concerns a loss of first love. How do you understand this word and what might it say about your own spiritual journey?

2. Are there times when you need to reset things to get back on track? How might that first love be restored?

3. Restorationist theologies suggest that something has been lost and needs to be restored. Looking at your place in the Christian community, do you see anything having been lost that needs to be restored? How might you participate in this act of restoration?

Reflection Questions for Congregations

1. The reading from Revelation 2 speaks to a congregation that has lost its first love. Looking at your congregation how might this word speak to it? How might it describe the way the church lives in the world? Why?

2. In the previous chapter, we looked at the role of Tradition in passing on the essence of the faith from generation to generation. Now we have looked at the concept of things being lost and restored. Looking at your congregation and perhaps denomination, what might have been lost over time that needs to be restored?

3. How might looking back to the founding visions enhance the congregation's vision of the future? How might that initial love be restored?

4

Embracing the Mission— The Evangelical Imperative

But you will receive power when the Holy Spirit has come upon you; and you will be my witnesses in Jerusalem, in all Judea and Samaria, and to the ends of the earth. —ACTS 1:6–11

EVERY EPISODE OF *STAR Trek: The Original Series* begins with Captain Kirk narrating the mission statement of the starship Enterprise: "Space, the final frontier. These are the voyages of the Starship Enterprise. Its five-year mission: to explore strange new worlds, to seek out new life and new civilizations, to boldly go where no man has gone before." When *Star Trek: The Next Generation* appeared twenty years later, the producers made a few changes to the statement. Instead of five years, the new crew embarked on a "continuing mission." They also replaced the words "no man" with "no one." Nevertheless, the crews (Enterprise old and new) still had a mission—to explore strange new worlds, seek out new life, and boldly go to new places.

The church is not exploring the far reaches of the galaxy (at least not yet), but it does have a "continuing mission" to "boldly go where no one has gone before." The words I want to emphasize here are "continuing" and "boldly." Our mission is rooted in one established by God long before any of us was born. That mission is the one given to Abraham and Sarah when they were called by God to bless the nations—through their descendants. This was also the mission embodied by Jesus, who reinterpreted that original covenant calling and then passed it on to his disciples. From there, the commission was passed on down through the centuries to us. The commission that Jesus gave his disciples, and through them to us, is simply this: "But you will receive power when the Holy Spirit has come upon you; and you will be my witnesses in Jerusalem, in all Judea and Samaria, and to the ends of the Earth" (Acts 1:8). Jesus tells the disciples that the Spirit will come upon them and give them all the power they will need to serve as his witnesses as the gospel moves out from Jerusalem to the ends of the earth. That is, they will have the boldness they'll need to accomplish this mission.

While the church's mission is a continuing one, I like the idea of five-year increments. When I arrived at my current congregation, I suggested that we envision our work together in five-year increments, which would be marked by sabbaticals. When I returned from my first sabbatical, I acknowledged the worlds that had been explored and the new forms of life that had been sought out as the church sought to boldly embrace the new adventures set before us by the Spirit. Looking forward, I suggested that the next phase would bring about its own new adventures in the Spirit. Putting things in those kinds of terms makes the mission more viable. We can handle five years at a time. Thinking in increments longer than five years can lead to a lot of anxiety.

For me, this missional imperative is rooted in my experiences within the evangelical community. I realize that the term "evangelical" has taken on unfortunate political connotations, and there is a lot of conversation among Evangelicals as to whether the term has become tainted. To be a white Evangelical, at least, is understood to embrace a narrowly conservative vision that rejects science, seeks to exclude immigrants from the United States (because they will dilute the white American Protestant majority), and opposes the full inclusion of one's LGBTQ neighbors in enjoying the full benefits of American society (not to mention being fully integrated into the faith community). There is truth to this description, but it's not the form of Evangelicalism that took root in my own life.[1]

For many today, at least in North America, the word "evangelical" has those political connotations I just mentioned, but more traditionally it has designated a conservative religious party that is orthodox in its doctrine and biblicist in its reading of the Bible (insists that the Bible is inerrant/infallible). That can lead to conservative positions regarding political and social issues (especially abortion and marriage equality), but not always. While American Evangelicalism is conservative in its theology and often in its social mores, the word "evangelical" can have a much broader meaning. In fact, in Europe to be evangelical is to be Protestant.

Before getting to the missional component of this understanding of Evangelicalism, I want to say something about the role of the Bible in my own journey as well as in Evangelicalism as a whole. It is true that "Evangelicals" affirm the normative authority of Scripture in matters of faith and practice, and often this confession is linked to an insistence that the Bible is inerrant (though not all Evangelicals endorse inerrancy, and even when affirming it, what this is understood to mean is that the Bible is inerrant in its original autographs, which no one currently has access to). An alternative to inerrancy suggests that Scripture is infallible (this is often understood to give more leeway in biblical interpretation). The idea here is that Scripture fulfills its purpose by providing an authoritative witness to the things of God, without adherents of this view believing that Scripture necessarily must be interpreted as being historically or scientifically accurate in all things. When I was in seminary in the 1980s, studying at a leading Evangelical seminary that had been under attack from more conservative Evangelicals for embracing infallibility over inerrancy, I discovered Karl Barth's teaching on the "threefold word of God." This formula puts the focus on the purpose of Scripture as a witness to Christ. Barth helped me embrace the normative witness of Scripture

---

1. For an account of leaving contemporary Evangelicalism that mirrors my own experience, see David Gushee's book *Still Christian*.

without being encumbered by having to make everything fit—like a jigsaw puzzle.[2]

What I discovered, as I was exposed to more historical-critical biblical scholarship, was that the issue isn't authority so as much as it is interpretation. Where Christians tend to disagree (and always have done so) has less to do with the status of Scripture as an authority as it does with the way we read it. This includes the cultural baggage we bring to the conversation. Fundamentalists are just as beholden to the Enlightenment as their liberal counterparts. With this in mind, we might be wise to heed the words of Saint Augustine, who wrote long before the contemporary debate over biblical inerrancy emerged: "And thus a man who is resting upon faith, hope and love, and who keeps a firm hold upon these, does not need the Scriptures except for the purpose of instructing others. Accordingly, many live without copies of the Scriptures, even in solitude, on the strength of these three graces."[3]

Although I believe that conversations about Scripture and its interpretation, as well as the nature of Christian doctrine, are important, for my purposes I want to lift up the missional dimension of the word "evangelical." What I mean here is that the evangelical imperative involves sharing the Christian message with the world in both word and deed (fulfilling in my mind that original calling given to Abraham and Sarah). That doesn't necessarily mean converting people from other religions to the Christian faith. Before we explore this dimension more fully, I need to acknowledge my own evangelical roots.

I am, first of all, a graduate twice over of a leading Evangelical seminary. It was because my spiritual journey has gone through the Evangelical movement that I sought to touch base with elements of it during my 2013 sabbatical. The primary way I did this was by making a pilgrimage to Fuller Theological Seminary, my educational home for nearly a decade. It was also a place where I have occasionally taught church history classes over the years. This visit to Fuller helped me reconnect with an important contributor

2. Cornwall, *Authority of Scripture.*
3. Augustine, *On Christian Doctrine*, bk. 1, ch. 39.

to my identity as a Christian. Among the contributions of this stop on my spiritual journey was the development of a deep and abiding appreciation of the Bible and its normative witness for the life of the church. I also gained an appreciation for the importance of sharing one's faith with the world (though I must acknowledge that the undergraduate courses on world missions that I took at Northwest Christian University prepared me for this conversation). As Jesus declared, "You are the light of the world. A city built on a hill cannot be hid. No one after lighting a lamp puts it under the bushel basket, but on the lampstand, and it gives light to all in the house. In the same way, let your light shine before others, so that they may see your good works and give glory to your Father in heaven" (Matt 5:14–16).

In terms of my overall journey, I may have joined the ranks of the "post-Evangelicals," but there are treasures that I continue to reclaim even as I've moved out from the core of the Evangelical movement. With that in mind, I can claim to be an Evangelical if we understand this word to involve proclaiming the good news of Jesus Christ to the world in word and deed. After all, the word "evangelical" derives from the Greek word that means good news, the word *euangelion.* Surely that is the calling given to the church whether it calls itself evangelical or not—proclaiming good news to the world so that the nations might be blessed.

We see this work of proclaiming the good news laid out in Matthew's Gospel. After his baptism in the Jordan by John, Jesus spent time in the wilderness, where his loyalty to the call of God was tested. He then retreated to his hometown in Galilee and stayed there until after the arrest of John. Then, Jesus went down to the Sea of Galilee and began preaching in towns like Capernaum. Like John before him, Jesus called on the people to repent (to turn around their lives) and commit their lives to the service of God, because the "Kingdom of Heaven has come near" (Matt 4:12–17). As Jesus went around the region preaching, he invited others to join him in this evangelical mission. He started by inviting four fishermen to leave their nets and the security of their employment to join him in the people-fishing business. Matthew tells us that

Jesus and his disciples went around Galilee "preaching the good news of the kingdom and curing every disease and every sickness among the people" (Matt 4:18–23). This is, once again, the evangelical imperative. It involves proclaiming the good news so that individuals and communities can experience the healing of body and soul.

We see this calling expressed by Second Isaiah, who speaks to the exiles in Babylon, giving them their divine commission. According to the prophet, God revealed to the exiles, "It is too light a thing that you should be my servant to raise up the tribes of Jacob and to restore the survivors of Israel; I will give you as a light to the nations, that my salvation may reach to the end of the earth" (Isa 49:6). This missional imperative is reflected in the mission statement of my denomination, which frames our calling in terms of being a "movement of wholeness in a fragmented world. As part of the one body of Christ, we welcome all to the Lord's Table as God has welcomed us." That seems in line with this evangelical calling, though as I read it in this context it seems a bit passive. It celebrates hospitality at the Lord's Table, but except for the word "movement," it does seem to lack the imperative to go out into the world with this message of wholeness. We share our reticence as a denomination about being too vocal about our faith commitments with much of Mainline Protestantism, which is unfortunate because I think we have good news to share.

When it comes to the missional imperative that I want to highlight here, one of its leading exponents in the eighteenth century was John Wesley. Along with his brother Charles, John Wesley helped found what became the Methodist movement. At one time, early in its history, Methodism was an expression of the evangelical wing of the Church of England. During my sabbatical trip to England in 2013, I had the opportunity to stop in at the Methodist Central Hall in London, where I had my picture taken with a life-sized statue of Wesley (he was not very tall). I bring up Wesley because he strongly believed that the church is called to reach beyond its walls and speak to the broader community that is often disconnected from what happens within the walls of the church.

He caused quite a stir in his day because he went out into the fields and public squares and preached to all who would listen. This was seen by many as undignified. Critics from within his own church spoke of his work in terms of "enthusiasm." We might take this as a positive commendation, but to his critics, especially among the bishops, it was anything but a compliment. Despite opposition, Wesley continued to pursue this evangelical vision because he believed the church had a missional calling (even if he didn't use these exact words). To be missional means that the church doesn't just engage in mission, but everything it is and does expresses this missional calling. While there is a place for maintenance in this calling, it can't be the main focus of a congregation's life.

Many mainline Protestants find the word "evangelism" rather off-putting. Perhaps this reticence about the word is that some may have been buttonholed at some point and had a religious message forced on them. This has led many moderate/liberal Christians to adopt the premise that religion is not only personal, but it is also a private affair. In other words, religion is something you do in the confines of your home or sacred space, but it shouldn't be expressed in the public square.

When I arrived at Central Woodward Christian Church in 2008, the church had been studying Martha Grace Reese's book *Unbinding the Gospel*. Then after I arrived, we continued to work with her books, sharing in a congregation-wide study of her follow-up book *Unbinding Your Heart*.[4] In these books, Reese has sought to help mainliners recover their public voice. Mainliners have become increasingly comfortable about speaking on justice issues but seem reticent about sharing the spiritual/religious foundations of that activism. We wonder why so many in our culture equate Christianity with more extremist perspectives. We've not been very good about sharing our understanding of the Christian faith. If we find our voice, we can discover that our missional calling is rooted in the Abrahamic call to participate in the ministry of blessing the nations.

---

4. Reese, *Unbinding the Gospel*; Reese, *Unbinding Your Heart*.

While some of the reticence is understandable, if we are to reclaim our founding visions it would be wise to give heed to the word we hear in the first chapter of the book of Acts. In this chapter, Luke gives an account of Jesus' final conversation with his followers. After the disciples ask him when he's going to "restore the kingdom to Israel," which suggests that at least some of his followers were still waiting for him to throw off Roman rule and reestablish the Davidic kingdom, Jesus quickly gives them a different sense of purpose. He tells them not to worry about such things. Instead, he speaks of an upcoming mission that will involve the reception of "power when the Holy Spirit has come upon you; and you will be my witnesses in Jerusalem, in all Judea and Samaria, and to the ends of the earth" (Acts 1:8).

The book of Acts is built on the principle espoused here in Acts 1:8. This verse functions much like the Great Commission of Matthew 28. Jesus tells the disciples that they will soon participate in a ministry of witness that will take them from Jerusalem to the ends of the earth. Before they take up this ministry, they will have to wait until the Spirit falls upon them, empowering them for this ministry of witness. This endowment of the Spirit comes as the community is gathered in an upper room on the day of Pentecost (Acts 2).

If you read the book of Acts with the eighth verse of chapter 1 as a guide, you will find that the church (mainly through the ministry of Paul) will bear witness to the message of Jesus, taking it from Jerusalem to Rome (is this the end of the earth in Luke's understanding?). Although the book of Acts concludes with Paul in a Roman jail, Luke seems to leave the story open so that those who come after him could continue writing this story. In doing this, the church continues to embrace the covenant calling made with Abraham and Sarah, that through their descendants the nations would be blessed.

If we use Acts 1:8 as a guideline for mission, we could compare our own community, where we live and do ministry, with Jerusalem. It is our starting point. We might see this first stop in terms of an old adage from the 1960s, which called people to "bloom where you are planted." I think I had a poster with those words on it up on the wall of my bedroom as a young teen. When I arrived at Central Woodward, I preached a sermon in which I suggested we might envision our Jerusalem as being that five-mile to ten-mile radius that branched out from our building. This would be our first point of missional contact—our local community. My idea was that this area warranted our first and greatest attention. This hasn't proven easy to do since the congregation was a transplant from Detroit with a membership that is spread over a wide area of Metro Detroit. Nevertheless, I believed (and still believe) that our local community, which includes the city of Troy and its environs, is our starting point. Nevertheless, while it is the starting point, it shouldn't be our total focus. A church's vision needs to include its neighborhood, but it can't be limited to it. With Jesus' commission as a guide, I suggested that we might reenvision Judea and Samaria as the broader metropolitan Detroit region as well as the state of Michigan (essentially our denominational region). With that in mind, over time we helped launch several ministries that extended across metropolitan Detroit and beyond. We helped launch a community organizing effort that, among other things, pushed the state housing authority to make designated federal funds available to those in need of assistance after a housing crash. We also helped launch a ministry in Detroit called Rippling Hope that helps homeowners with minor repairs, boards up abandoned building, cleans vacant lots, and more. We reenvisioned these ministries and others that preexisted my arrival, in terms of a missional calling. But the mission statement doesn't end with the state boundary. Jesus had a much larger vision that extended to the ends of the earth, and thus our vision as the church should include that larger vision so that the nations might be blessed (as the covenant with Abraham and Sarah envisioned). Wherever it is that God has placed us, we have the opportunity to embrace God's mission. In doing this we reclaim our founding vision, and in doing this we become evangelicals—in the broad sense, not the party sense.

I bring this conversation to a close by sharing the words from a Charles Wesley hymn. It's not one of his more famous hymns, and so you won't find it in most hymnals. The words might even sound a bit dated, but I think they capture the evangelical spirit to which we're called to embrace:

> When first sent forth to minister the word,
> Say, did we preach ourselves, or Christ the Lord?
> Was it our aim disciples to collect,
> To raise a party, or to found a sect?
> No; but to spread the power of Jesus' name,
> Repair the walls of our Jerusalem,
> Revive the piety of ancient days,
> And fill the earth with our Redeemer's praise.[5]

Reflection Questions for Individuals

1. What does the word "evangelical" mean to you? What is its meaning in our time? As discussed in this chapter, how might this word be understood and perhaps reclaimed?

2. How might we understand the role of the Bible in the life of the church? What authority does it have, and how might we engage it in the twenty-first century?

3. How might you participate in the mission of God in the world? What might this involve?

Reflection Questions for Congregations

1. If we understand the evangelical imperative in missional terms, how would you define the mission of the congregation? What role does evangelism play in that mission?

2. How does Scripture inform the mission of the congregation? What role does it play in discerning the mission of the church? With that in mind, how do you read Jesus' commission in Acts 1:8? How does it inform your vision of ministry in the community and the world?

5. Quoted in Chilcote, *Recapturing the Wesleys' Vision*, 99.

3. In this chapter, the author suggests the benefit of planning in five-year increments. How might the congregation envision the path forward in mission? If Tradition and restoration look back, how does the church look forward?

5

Room to Move—The Call to Freedom

For you were called to freedom, brothers and sisters, only do not use
your freedom as an opportunity for self-indulgence, but through love
become slaves to one another. For the whole law is summed up in
a single commandment, "You shall love your neighbor as yourself."
—GALATIANS 5:13–14

PAUL OPENS CHAPTER 5 of his Galatian letter with the words, "For
freedom Christ has set us free. Stand firm, therefore, and do not
submit again to a yoke of slavery" (Gal 5:1). That word concerning freedom has a certain appeal to an American context in which
freedom has been hailed as a core value. While freedom has been a
defining concept for Americans, the nation tolerated slavery from
its founding until a bloody Civil War ended the practice. Even then
true freedom wasn't realized for most of America's former slaves.
They were not alone. It is important to remember that women did
not achieve the right to vote until the 1920s, Native Americans
were pushed off their lands and onto reservations, often far from
their homelands, and immigrants from Asia were not allowed to
become citizens until well into the twentieth century. Therefore,
freedom is not something to be taken for granted even in the "land
of the free."

Paul writes to the Galatian church and tells them not to allow others to enslave them. This word was delivered to gentile Christians, who were caught in the middle of a conflict between two groups of Jewish-Christian interpreters of Israel's heritage. Paul understood his mission as being rooted in a "new covenant," a concept that has deep biblical roots (Jer 31:31–34). Richard Hays writes that "the new covenant does not overturn and renounce the old; rather, in the new covenant God writes the Law on the hearts of the people and restores them to a relationship with him that they had broken through their unfaithfulness. It constitutes an internalizing and renewal of the old covenant."[1] As for Paul's word about freedom here, Hays writes that "the crucial indicator of that fact is that freedom in Christ manifests itself through the formation of concrete communities where the old barriers of nation, race, and gender are overcome in communities at the one table (cf. 3:26–29; 5:13–15). In short, the freedom Paul proclaims is an *ecclesial* freedom; it is to be embodied in the corporate life of the church, as Gal 5:13—6:10 will make clear."[2] The freedom that Paul envisions is different from what we might envision, especially those of us who live in Western democracies. This is not an invitation to complete autonomy or individualism. Instead, it is community-centered.

It is to this community that Paul offers a pathway of blessing, in line with the promise given to Abraham. The main issue in this debate was circumcision, which was a marker of identity. Paul said this marker was not needed for those who were not Abraham's direct descendants. So how might we hear this invitation to experience freedom in Christ today? What might we be free from? What could enslave us?

As we consider these questions, we hear a caveat to this offer of freedom in Christ. While we all wish to be free, freedom comes in different forms. With that in mind, Paul tells the Galatian church not to use their freedom "as an opportunity for self-indulgence, but through love become slaves to one another"

1. Hays, "Letter to the Galatians," 308.
2. Hays, "Letter to the Galatians," 310.

(Gal 5:13). As I noted earlier, the issue at hand is circumcision. This was an important question facing the early church. As the Christian movement, which is rooted in Judaism, spread among gentiles (non-Jews), the church wrestled with the extent to which these new converts should be expected to follow Jewish practices, especially concerning dietary laws and circumcision. Paul's answer to the question was that male converts need not be circumcised, removing a major cultural impediment to conversion.

As I think about this debate in the Galatian church, my mind goes to the practices of missionaries who sought to impose Western "civilization" on those whom they evangelized. Not only did the missionaries share a word about Jesus, but they required their converts to wear Western-style clothes and adopt other Western/ European cultural conventions. Even today we wrestle with the question of assimilation. As the gospel crosses cultures, how does it become embodied? For example, must one leave behind Hinduism to embrace Jesus? Those who participate in the *Khrist bhaktas* movement have chosen to embrace both. Is this syncretism? Or is it simply a culturally relevant way of following Jesus without leaving behind one's culture? These questions continue to face the church as it wrestles with what kinds of fences might be erected.[3] At the same time, as Paul reminds the Galatians that freedom doesn't mean self-indulgence. Instead, "serve each other in love. All the Law has been fulfilled in a single statement: *Love your neighbor as yourself*" (Gal 5:13–14, CEB).

I hear this word about freedom in light of my many years as a Disciples of Christ pastor. From the earliest days of the Stone-Campbell Movement—my own denomination, the Christian Church (Disciples of Christ), represents one of three major branches of this movement—Disciples have valued the principle of freedom.[4] It's one of the reasons why I embraced this tradition. It has allowed me to bring together the various strands of my rather circuitous spiritual journey into a single whole.

---

3. Duerksen and Dyrness, *Seeking Church*, 132–34.

4. Cornwall, *Freedom in Covenant*, 1–10.

The role that freedom plays in the heritage of the Stone-Campbell/Disciples movement is rooted in its birth on the American frontier soon after the nation's founding. The movement was born during the presidencies of Thomas Jefferson and James Madison, at a time when many European Americans took advantage of the nation's expanding borders to roam westward. If your neighbor got too close, you could always move further out into the wilderness. This was also the era of the Second Great Awakening, which produced significant movements, especially among Baptists, Methodists, and some Presbyterians. As the frontier expanded west, Christian denominations planted churches, and the denominations that offered the most flexibility in terms of doctrine and institutional structure were the ones that thrived in this new environment. The Stone-Campbell Movement, which began life in the frontier regions of Western Pennsylvania, Kentucky, Ohio, and what is now the panhandle of West Virginia, was one of these more adaptable traditions and it thrived on the frontier.

The message preached by the Christians (Barton Stone) and the Disciples (Alexander Campbell) focused on a simple creed: Christ is the center, and Scripture (especially the New Testament) is the normative guide. This vision is best summed up in a slogan that the founders borrowed from the seventeenth-century church leader Rupertus Meldenius: "In essentials unity, in opinions liberty, in all things charity." While this statement is a powerful call to find common ground, determining the essentials upon which we will unite has never been easy, which makes the third point of great import. Charity or love is necessary if we are to navigate our differences on matters of faith and practice.

Democracy isn't really a biblical concept. There were ancient examples of democracy in places like Athens, but biblical writers tended to speak in terms of monarchy, especially the monarchy of God. Nevertheless, while our modern forms of democracy don't have biblical foundations, you can't blame a person like Alexander Campbell, in the heady days of the new American republic, for finding democracy present in the biblical story. Like many of his day, he embraced the democratic principles that prevailed on the frontier. He believed that they held the key to bringing about unity and spreading the gospel across the nation. He wrote, "It is not possible, or, in other words, it is not in human nature, to love liberty, freedom of thought, of speech and of action, in the state, and to hate it in the church; or to love it in the church and to hate it in the state."[5] You can't value freedom in the nation and hate it in the church. Understandably, this was an idea that bore fruit in the early days of the nineteenth century.

Thomas and Alexander Campbell, as well as Barton Stone, concluded that the unity they sought required freedom. In their estimation, this freedom necessitated abandoning the use of creeds as tests of fellowship. Now, they didn't completely reject the creeds, they just didn't think creeds should be used to exclude people from the community. In their minds, creeds and other statements of faith had value only if understood to be signposts that illustrated the journey that Christians have taken from the first century to the present. Whatever the creeds declared had to be assessed as to how they agreed with the superior authority of the New Testament. While the nation set up a legal system to interpret the Constitution, these early Disciple leaders took a more radical step and insisted that every Christian had the freedom to interpret the Bible for themselves. Or, to put it differently, one should let the Bible speak for itself.

This gift of freedom entails a great deal of risk. People may claim freedom for themselves and not extend it to others. Still others might rush headlong into hedonism, doing whatever comes naturally (at most they would adopt the principle of "do no harm"). It's worth remembering that while the promise of freedom and equality are enshrined in the Declaration of Independence, many of those who signed the document, including the primary author of that document, owned slaves. It would take nearly a century before the nation rid itself of this stain, and even after fighting a devastating Civil War that ended slavery, true freedom remained a dream for many. So, simply proclaiming the importance of

---

5. Quoted in Osborn, *Experiment in Liberty*, 25.

freedom doesn't mean one lives out the principle, whether in the nation or the church.

Abraham Lincoln may not have been a perfect vessel (he shared many of the racist sentiments of his fellow Euro-American compatriots), but he understood that a nation committed to freedom couldn't survive if it was half-slave and half-free. Lincoln rooted his vision for the nation in the Declaration of Independence. He believed that this document provided the founding vision for the nation, and so when he gave his "Gettysburg Address" he returned to this founding vision and reclaimed for a divided nation its promise of freedom and equality for all.

There is another source of Lincoln's understanding of freedom—his reading of Scripture. Lincoln never joined a church, but he was an avid reader of the Bible and he regularly attended Presbyterian churches. As to why he never joined a church, Lincoln replied that he would join the first church that made as its sole qualification for membership Jesus' summation of the Law: that we should love God with our heart, soul, and mind, and love our neighbor as we love ourselves. One of my predecessors at Central Woodward, Edgar DeWitt Jones, was an avid student of Lincoln's life. He shared this word in a sermon: "It may be said by way of comment on this quotation that the statement of Jesus with respect to the law and the gospel is written on the altars of all the churches, but so much else is also written there that is secondary and relatively unimportant that the fundamental teachings of Jesus are obscured."[6]

How might our doctrines and practices obscure the fundamental teachings of Jesus? That is a good question to consider if we're intent on reaffirming founding principles for our churches and our spiritual lives.

The founders of the Stone-Campbell Movement dedicated themselves to removing as much of the stuff from church life that they believed obscured the biblical message as they could (their restorationist impulse). They weren't completely successful, but their commitment to freedom of interpretation serves as

6. Jones, *Sermons I Love to Preach*, 141.

a reminder of the value of regularly cleaning out one's theological closet. Once that occurs, it is possible to reset one's vision to the vision laid out in God's covenant with Abraham and Sarah and developed further by Jesus.

Yes, we are free in Christ. As Paul told the Galatian church, which was struggling with standards for membership, "For freedom Christ has set us free. Stand firm therefore and do not submit again to the yoke of slavery" (Gal 5:1).

Jesus set his disciples free for the mission of the kingdom. Being numbered among these disciples, we have been invited to follow him and bring the good news of God's realm to the world. There is freedom here to explore matters of faith and to learn what it means to be a follower of Jesus. When Lincoln laid out his own creed, he sought one that could unite rather than divide. That is, I believe, a founding vision embraced by the early adherents of the Stone-Campbell Movement two centuries back.

In most Disciples churches, membership in the congregation is based on the affirmation of a simple confession that Jesus is the Christ, the Son of God, and that one accepts Jesus as Lord and Savior. As you can see, this simple creed leaves room to roam. Some of those in a congregation of this sort might take a more minimalist view, and others a more expansive one, but whether one has a low Christology or a high Christology, all are considered to be one in Christ.

As this is in part the exploration of a personal spiritual journey, I can say that one of the reasons why I ended up as a Disciple was this commitment to freedom. I appreciate the room that this tradition provides for persons to roam theologically. Freedom to roam doesn't mean that there are no limits. Two people can have different understandings of Jesus' identity and still be Disciples, but Jesus has to fit somewhere in one's confession of faith. It is common for new members to be asked to affirm the confession that Jesus is the Christ, the Son of God (Matt 16:16). We may have differences in how we read this declaration, but we are united in this confession as members of a Christian community that often includes people with differing theologies and politics. Yes, "In essentials unity, in opinions liberty, in all things charity."

While Christians can claim to be free in Christ, with this freedom comes responsibility. Paul tells the Galatian church to "not use your freedom as an opportunity for self-indulgence, but through love become slaves to one another" (Gal 5:13). The freedom one has in Christ is circumscribed by the call to love one's neighbor as one's self, which is the way of Jesus and the foundation of true freedom.

It is good to remember that the freedom of the Christian is rooted in the law of the Lord. Neither Paul nor Jesus threw out the Torah, but they did seek to understand Torah as the means, not the goal. Making the law the goal is to be entrapped by legalism. However, in avoiding the trap one shouldn't fall victim to the trap of libertinism. As Paul reminded the Corinthians, while all things are lawful, not all things are profitable (1 Cor 10:23).

One of the paradoxes of the Christian faith is the simultaneous message of freedom and the call to be slaves to one another. In trying to make sense of this paradox, we might turn to Richard Rohr, who writes, "The reason we can move toward real freedom is because we started with moral laws and clear expectations from authority figures, which put good and needed limits to our natural egocentricity."[7] When we were children, our parents set boundaries for us. As we matured, we gained more and more freedom. No responsible parent hands the keys to the family car to a five-year-old child. Paul spoke of the law being our tutor so that we might know the difference between what is appropriate and what is not. But to be in Christ is to be freed from these constraints (Gal 3:24–25). The training wheels can be set aside.

Ultimately, the way we exercise our freedom in Christ is constrained by the law of love, both love of God and of neighbor. Upon these two commandments, Jesus declared, "hang all the Law and the Prophets" (Matt 22:34–40). If we embrace this vision, which is the inheritance Jesus shares with his followers, then we will become agents of blessing to the nations. In other words,

---

7. Rohr, *Things Hidden*, 80.

freedom isn't the goal either. It is the blessing of God that we seek to share in.

Reflection Questions for Individuals

1. What does it mean to be free in Christ? What are the constraints that might be placed on your freedom?

2. If freedom is ours in Christ, what does that mean for what or how we believe or behave? Do creeds or other faith or behavior statements interfere with this freedom? Why do you think this way?

3. What role does love play in living in freedom? Why?

Reflection Questions for Congregations

1. How is freedom to be understood in a congregational context? How is it expressed?

2. How are matters of theology and behavior addressed if freedom in Christ is a core value? Does this preclude or allow for the use of creedal statements? Why or why not?

3. The principle espoused by Rupert Meldenius is "In essentials unity, in nonessentials liberty, in all things liberty." How might this principle guide the life of the church? What are the challenges of implementing such a vision? Why?

6

A People Empowered—
A Pentecostal Gift

Now there are varieties of gifts, but the same Spirit; and there are
varieties of services, but the same Lord; and there are varieties
of activities, but it is the same God who activates all of them in
everyone. To each is given the manifestation of the Spirit for the
common good. . . . All these are activated by one and the same Spirit,
who allots to each one individually just as the Spirit chooses.
—1 CORINTHIANS 12:4–7, 11

WHEN A STORM HITS, knocking out the power, life can get
interesting. No lights, no refrigeration, no stove, no heat, and no
television or computer. If you have a smartphone you might have
access to the outside world, but if you don't, you're in the dark.
And that's not a happy feeling. Power comes in many forms. It can
be used to bless, and it can corrupt, and it can be used to destroy.
For example, the same atomic elements used to create electricity
can be used to build bombs that can destroy cities and nations.

Although power can be dangerous, it's also essential to life. In
this chapter, I'd like to affirm the idea that there is power that comes
to us from God through the Holy Spirit and that by embracing it

we are better equipped to share in this ministry of blessing the nations, which is the founding vision given to Abraham and Sarah.

Christian journalist Andy Crouch wrote a book about "redeeming the gift of power." Crouch wrote that "power is for flourishing—teeming, fruitful, multiplying abundance."[1] That is, because God uses the power of creation to shape where life can flourish, we who bear the image of God get to participate with God in creating these kinds of environments. Is not flourishing similar to blessing? Miroslav Volf also speaks of the important contribution religion makes to human flourishing and flourishing in general.

> I consider God's relation to human beings and human beings' relation to God to be the condition of possibility for human life and flourishing in all dimensions. I believe that faith and politics are two distinct cultural systems but that an authentic faith is always engaged, at work to relieve personal suffering as well as to push against social injustice, political violence, and environmental degradation.[2]

I've noted that my denomination has envisioned its identity in terms of being a "movement of wholeness in a fragmented world." This call to participate in a work of God that leads to the flourishing of creation, including the human creation, seems to fit with this denominational calling as well. It also fits with the founding vision given to Abraham and Sarah, which commissioned them and their descendants to be a means of blessing to the peoples of the earth. The question is, how does this occur? How are we empowered to fulfill this calling?

As we explore the nature of power, we might want to ask the question of whether there are some things God cannot do. For instance, can God prevent evil from taking place without our participation? That is, if we affirm the principle that God is by God's very nature love, and that this love is by definition uncontrolling

1. Crouch, *Playing God*, 35.
2. Volf, *Flourishing*, 9.

and non-coercive, then how does power express itself? Might we say that God empowers, but not overpowers?[3]

In Acts 1, Jesus told the disciples that they "would receive power when the Holy Spirit has come upon you." That power came upon them, according to Acts 2, on the day of Pentecost. When this outpouring of the Spirit took place, the community was prepared. They were waiting for the Spirit to come upon them. They might not have known all this entailed, but they had received the promise of Jesus that the Spirit would come upon them so that they might proclaim the good news to the ends of the earth, beginning in Jerusalem (Acts 1:8). So, as they waited in the upper room, the Spirit of God came upon them like a mighty wind. This empowering presence of the Spirit enabled the people to proclaim the good news of Jesus in languages known to the hearers below, but unknown to the speakers. When the people in the city heard these things, they asked Peter, "What must we do to be saved?" He answered, "Repent, and be baptized, every one of you so that your sins may be forgiven, and you will receive the gift of the Holy Spirit" (Acts 2:38). In other words, he told them to turn back to God and be baptized as a sign of that repentance, which would lead to the reception of forgiveness and the gift of the Holy Spirit. Many responded positively to this invitation. Then, with fits and starts, the mission moved outward into the world, embodied in the ministry of Paul.

What is the purpose of this gift of power that comes with the presence of the Holy Spirit? That's the question Paul tries to answer in 1 Corinthians 12–14. Paul deals with this question in the context of a congregation that is out of control. Members of this community were focusing on their own spiritual experiences. In doing this, they stepped on their neighbors. Paul didn't reject these experiences of the spirit, but he put them in context. Paul wrote to his friends in Corinth, reminding them that the church is the body of Christ and that each member of the church is an important part of that body. Each of them, as is true of us, was given a gift, as the Spirit chooses so that they and we can praise God and serve

3. Oord, *God Can't*, 176. Oord, *Uncontrolling Love of God*, 116.

and love our neighbors. There is a diversity of giftedness because a variety of gifts are needed to create an environment where life can flourish.[4]

Although Barton Stone hosted the Cane Ridge Revival, where ecstatic experiences were commonplace, the denominational tradition which he helped create (the Disciples of Christ) has tended to emphasize the rational side of the Christian faith. The message that was broadcast by this movement was that you don't have to rely on ecstatic experiences as proof that you belong to God; just remember your baptism. Besides, when it comes to knowing the will of God we need no other source besides Scripture (and the interpretive power of our intellect). There is much in this to commend. It was one of the reasons I was originally attracted to the movement in college. It also can be a very encouraging message for people who lack "spiritual experiences." Even though Alexander Campbell appears to have had a life-altering spiritual experience during a shipwreck, he didn't universalize that experience.

I spent time during my late teens through my college years in the International Church of the Foursquare Gospel (a Pentecostal denomination founded by healing evangelist Aimee Semple McPherson). I left this tradition at the end of my senior year of college and eventually found my way into the Christian Church (Disciples of Christ), a denomination connected to my college. My reason for migrating from Pentecostalism to the Disciples had a lot to do with the Disciples' emphasis on the rational side of the Christian faith. While this emphasis fits my personality, you can take a person out of a movement, but that doesn't mean the movement didn't leave its mark on you as a person. This is a central reason why I decided to write a book about spiritual gifts.

I didn't realize how deep the seed had been planted until I engaged in a conversation with Amos Yong in 2012. He had come to my church to give a set of presentations and we were talking about the manuscript for my book on spiritual gifts, which I had asked him to read over. In the course of the conversation, Amos asked me why I spoke of myself as an ex-Pentecostal. If I still affirmed

4. See Cornwall, *Unfettered Spirit*, 159–62.

the basic premise that the Spirit of God empowered us for service, why use the prefix "ex" to describe myself? Amos's question made sense and I no longer speak of myself as an ex-Pentecostal. I have reclaimed this founding dimension of my life that is rooted in the promise of Pentecost. That doesn't mean I've embraced everything that goes with this movement, but I have reclaimed the treasure that is the Pentecostal embrace of the work of the Spirit in the life of the church and the lives of individual Christians (and likely beyond the Christian community).

So, even as my Anglican heritage and my sojourn in Evangelicalism left their mark on me, my sojourn within Pentecostalism also contributed to my "spiritual DNA." As I planned for my sabbatical in the fall of 2013, I decided to spend time reflecting on this inheritance. This included making a pilgrimage to Angelus Temple, the mother church of the Foursquare Gospel denomination. We were fortunate to find someone at the church who let us in to see the sanctuary (it had changed significantly since my last visit). I realize that not everyone experiences church buildings in the same way I do, but it was spiritually empowering to be in that space and to think about the ministry of Aimee Semple McPherson, a person who has long fascinated me. Then Cheryl and I visited the Foursquare Heritage Center next door. We had a great time talking with the docent at the center, which was located in what had been Sister Aimee's parsonage. During our visit with the docent, we talked about Sister Aimee and her church, as well as its influence on life in Southern California.

Sister Aimee was a complicated person, which is perhaps why I find her story so fascinating. In an age when women were largely excluded from the pulpit, even in more liberal denominations, it took a person like her to push through the barriers that both church and society placed in the way of women. Believing that God had called her to preach, and that she could do nothing other than preach, she broke through barriers and became one of the most powerful religious figures of her day. She was charismatic and dramatic, and she drew people of all types into the community of faith. While my own theology differs from hers, I think it is important to acknowledge that she accomplished some amazing things. I always love to tell the story of how Aimee Semple McPherson's church fed more people during the Great Depression than did the county of Los Angeles. I think this is a sign of spiritual empowerment. Although I left this Pentecostal denomination while in my early twenties and have often struggled with integrating my Pentecostal inheritance into my spiritual life, I give thanks for friends like Amos Yong and Ray Wheeler who have helped me reintegrate that portion of my life into my ongoing journey in the company of the Spirit.

It was this early experience with Foursquare churches that introduced me to the concept of spiritual gifts (I don't remember any conversations about spiritual gifts in my Episcopal Sunday school). It led me to consider carefully Paul's words about the variety of gifts or *charismata* that enable us to fulfill our callings as Christians. I discovered that while there might be a variety of gifts, there is only one Spirit who gives to each the gift(s) one needs to fulfill this calling. Thus, while the word "charismatic" might be assigned to a particular group of Christians, I concluded that perhaps we're all charismatics. In making this claim, I rest my case on the assumption that if we are in Christ then we have received the gift of the Holy Spirit, which brings with it the power of the Spirit and gifts for service to God and to our neighbors, both near and far.

I want to return for a moment to this Pentecostal movement that helped form me. Some would trace the modern Pentecostal movement to the ministry of Charles Parham, a Holiness preacher, at whose Bible school in 1901 it is said that the gift of speaking in tongues as the initial evidence of the Spirit's presence was experienced. Although Parham plays an important role in this story, the Azusa Street Revival of 1906 is now thought to be the true beginning of the movement. It was from Azusa Street in Los Angeles that the movement began to spread exponentially. Standing at the center of this revival was an African American Holiness preacher named William Seymour. He had begun holding meetings in a storefront church located on Azusa Street that began to gather people who had ecstatic experiences, which they attributed to the Holy Spirit. People spoke in tongues, experienced healing, and witnessed other miraculous events. Many of the participants began to believe that their experiences were signs that the world was entering the last days. They came to believe that the Spirit was again moving in the world, just like on the day of Pentecost. Surely God was at work in their midst. They saw themselves, at least at first, as a vanguard of renewal for the church. Of course, not everyone received their witness, and so they began to develop their own networks outside the mainstream churches. That is until the Charismatic movement broke out in Mainline Protestant and Roman Catholic churches during the 1960s.

Unfortunately, the birth of the Charismatic movement led to division within these mainstream churches. People on both sides of the Pentecostal divide began to see themselves as superior to the other. Because of this, the possibilities of learning from each other were squandered. Eventually, things settled down and people outside the Pentecostal movement began to discover Paul's teachings on spiritual gifts, which led to new opportunities for mutual encouragement and cross-pollination.

One of the gifts that the early Pentecostal movement brought to the broader church was the inclusive nature of these early revivals. In 1906 the American church was largely segregated along racial/ethnic lines, but at Azusa Street people from every ethnic group gathered to worship and hear this black preacher teach the word of God. While most of the participants were poor and lower middle class, the revival crossed socioeconomic lines as well. Besides, at a time when even liberal Protestant churches continued to bar women from entering their pulpits and administering the sacraments, this movement allowed women to preach. Yes, the message William Seymour offered was one of radical egalitarianism.[5] Unfortunately, as time wore on much of this egalitarianism was set aside. Nevertheless, you can imagine why many good upstanding Christians viewed this revival with suspicion and even disdain. It was dangerous!

5. Espinoza, "Ordinary Prophet," 41–43.

So, an important element of this encounter with the Spirit at Azusa Street was its impetus toward breaking through social and cultural barriers. Amos Yong notes that "Seymour understood the reconciliation of races as made possible by the cross of Christ but actualized through the outpouring of the Spirit."[6] The late Church of God in Christ leader Ithiel Clemmons observed this about Seymour's founding vision as it was expressed at Azusa Street: "Seymour championed one doctrine above all others: There must be no color line or any other division of the Church of Jesus Christ because God is no respecter of persons. . . . This inclusive fellowship is not a human construct but a divine glossolalic community of human equality. Spiritual power sprang more from interracial equality than from glossolalia."[7] If we are to live in the power of the Spirit then our lives and our ministries will be expressed through standing with those on the margins and those who have been disempowered by society. For me this has involved a variety of activities from my interfaith work, partnering with colleagues and congregations that are non-white, and being an ally to women clergy and LGBTQ persons. While I'm not sure Seymour would share all of my passions, I find in his vision the foundation for ministries of justice and peace that are expressions of the founding vision given to Abraham and Sarah of being a blessing to the nations.

The founding vision of the church is this: God made a covenant with Abraham and Sarah, telling them that the nations would be blessed through their descendants. Among these descendants was Jesus, who embodied the covenant and then passed on to his disciples this covenant promise. They passed that promise on to their descendants, and then down through ages until it reached us, making us heirs of this promise. The message we hear in Acts and 1 Corinthians is that through the Spirit, God has gifted us and empowered us to carry out this mission. These gifts of God are "manifestations of the Spirit for the common good."

6. Yong, *Spirit Poured Out*, 72.
7. Quoted in Yong, *Spirit Poured Out*, 72.

When it comes to deciding when and where the Spirit comes into our lives, Scripture offers several pictures. It might be baptism, or it might be some other subsequent event. Although we've been focusing on the call of Abraham and Sarah, when it comes to the empowering presence of the Spirit we can go back to Genesis 2, where God, having created the earth, takes some dirt and fashions it into a body, into which God breathes life. In Hebrew, that breath of life is known as *ruach*, which can be translated as "wind," as "breath," and as "spirit." So maybe what God provides at this point in the creation story is "spirit-breath" (Gen 2:7). That is, the Spirit of God indwells us from birth, and therefore the gifts of God are already present within us from the very beginning of our lives. Grace Ji-Sun Kim adds to this picture the idea of vibration, pointing to the effects of the Spirit hovering over the abyss at the moment of creation (Gen 2:2). She writes that "all created matter vibrates, as created matter is never static. As living things vibrate, we are reminded that the Spirit initiated this vibration and has allowed all created things to vibrate."[8] We simply have to nurture this spirit that is present within us and around us, so that the gifts of God can be used to bring blessing to all.

This embrace of the Spirit that the Pentecostal Revival sparked might also be the foundation for the kind of interfaith engagement many of us in the Christian community have embraced. Because, as Amos Yong has suggested, in our interfaith engagements Christology often leads to an impasse, perhaps embracing a pneumatological approach will prove more fruitful. That doesn't mean we neglect Christology, but by starting with the Spirit we might find more productive pathways to engagement. Yong writes that "a pneumatological theology of religions may, in fact, assist in reducing feelings of religious or cultural superiority vis-á-vis those in other faiths and promote a more humble and Christ-like attitude, thereby allowing genuine interreligious communication and the sharing of the Gospel to proceed."[9] Grace Ji-Sun Kim takes this a step further and asks, "If Yahweh's Spirit is present everywhere

8. Kim, *Reimagining Spirit*, 92.
9. Yong, *Discerning the Spirit(s)*, 63.

and experienced everywhere, could it be the same Spirit that is recognized in other cultures but simply named differently?"[10] By bringing the Spirit more fully into view, perhaps we might find a path toward a deeper engagement with our neighbors whose religious commitments are different from our own. That doesn't mean we don't reside fully within our faith, but we might see God working in places and ways we hadn't expected. After all, the Spirit is unfettered.

Reflection Questions for Individuals

1. What is your understanding of the role of the Spirit in the life of the church?

2. Have you engaged in a process of discovery of spiritual gifts? If so, what did you discover? Does this make sense of your own experience?

3. How should we understand spiritual power in light of a theology of giftedness? How might it be expressed?

Reflection Questions for Congregations

1. How is power understood and expressed in the life of the congregation? Is it egalitarian or hierarchical or something in between?

2. How does your congregation understand the role of the Holy Spirit in its midst? Do you have a theology of spiritual gifts? How is this understood and expressed in the life of the congregation, especially in relation to church leadership?

3. The earliest Pentecostal revival at Azusa Street was diverse in its leadership and participation. How might a theology of spiritual gifts enhance diversity in the life of the church? How might it contribute to a congregation's embrace of social justice and liberation?

10. Kim, *Reimagining Spirit*, 74.

4. Following up on the previous question, how might our engagement with the Spirit of God and the gifts of the Spirit enable deeper interfaith engagement?

7

How Blessed It Is to Live in Unity— An Ecumenical Vision

How very good and pleasant it is
 when kindred live together in unity!
It is like the precious oil on the head,
 running down upon the beard,
on the beard of Aaron,
 running down over the collar of his robes.
It is like the dew of Hermon,
 which falls on the mountains of Zion.
For there the Lord ordained his blessing,
 life forevermore. —PSALM 133

THE ORIGINAL MOTTO OF the United States was *E Pluribus Unum*, "out of the many, one." This motto, which unfortunately was never codified as the official motto of the nation, affirms the principle that even though this is a diverse nation it is also one nation. This principle is important to the future of the United States because it is becoming increasingly diverse racially, ethnically, and religiously. We are near the tipping point when no particular ethnic/ racial group will claim more than 50 percent of the population. For some, this is a rather scary proposition (leading to anti-immigrant activism—which isn't a new reality in the United States, unfortunately), but for others, this is the natural outcome of being a nation built by a combination of immigrants, descendants of slaves, and indigenous inhabitants. The truth is that some of the contributors to this diversity have not been as valued as others, as seen in Jim Crow, the reservation system, and laws that excluded Asians from citizenship and thus residency. The list could go on. We face the challenge as a society of discovering how we can achieve some sense of unity while affirming the increasing diversity in our midst. This will require us to recognize that not all forms of unity are equal. The word "assimilation" is often heard when the topic of diversity comes up. It's a bit like the word "color-blind." Both words assume that unity in diversity involves those whose ethnicity or culture differs from the majority should conform to the mores of the majority. In the case of the United States, assimilation assumes whiteness. However, moving forward, unity can't be defined by conformity to white Euro-centric cultural practices. It may be difficult to envision true pluralism, but that is a path that we'll need to take if we're to experience any sense of unity without uniformity.

What is true of the nation can be said of the church. Taken as a whole, the church is diverse in age, ethnicity, gender, politics, and theology. At the same time, if you are so inclined to recite the Apostles' Creed, you will declare this is "*one,* holy, catholic, and apostolic church." That unity brings blessings is affirmed by the psalmist, who compares unity among sisters and brothers to precious oil running down the beard of the priest. Too often this unity that the psalmist prizes is understood in terms of uniformity, but this needn't be the case. However, finding true unity in true diversity will not be easy.

I am an ordained minister in a Christian tradition that has made unity a hallmark of our movement. Barton Stone, one of the founders of this movement, declared that unity should be our "polar star." Thomas Campbell, another founder, declared that the "Church of Christ upon earth is essentially, intentionally, and constitutionally one; consisting of all those in every place that profess their faith in Christ and obedience to him in all things according to the Scriptures."[1] Campbell and Stone were committed to the cause of Christian unity because they believed disunity among Christians disrupted the mission of God. As a result, they committed themselves to rectifying that situation. Alexander Campbell, son of Thomas, who is also considered a founder of the movement, offered two principles as the basis of Christian unity:

> 1st. *Nothing is essential to the conversion of the world but the union and co-operation of Christians.*
> 2d. *Nothing is essential to the union of Christians but the Apostle's teaching or testimony.*[2]

As you can see, Alexander Campbell linked the conversion of the world to union in Christ and based this union in the apostle's teaching, by which he meant the New Testament. For him, unity would come as the church returned to its founding principles, which he called the "ancient order of things." Thus, if the founding vision of the church is to bring blessing (good news) to the nations, then our divisions and schisms will serve as a distraction. They are like a loud noise that keeps people from hearing and experiencing the good news of Jesus.

This call to Christian unity has long been a central focus of my life and ministry. That's probably because my spiritual journey has taken me into a variety of denominational traditions. I've been an Episcopalian, Pentecostal, Baptist, Presbyterian, Evangelical Covenant, and two varieties of the Stone-Campbell Movement (while developing strong friendships with members of the third branch). As a result, I often feel more at home in an ecumenical context, and even an interfaith context, than a denominational one. So, the message that Stone and the Campbells proclaimed resonates with me.

The call to unity is also an important legacy of the congregation I serve. Edgar Dewitt Jones, the pastor who defined the identity of this congregation during his long tenure with the church, was deeply involved in the ecumenical movement of his

1. Campbell, "Declaration and Address," 18.
2. Campbell, *Christian System*, 107.

day both locally and nationally. He served for a time as president of the Association for the Promotion of Christian Unity, which was the predecessor of the denomination's Christian Unity and Interfaith Ministries (of which I am a board member). At a later date, he served as president of the Federal Council of Churches, the forerunner of the National Council of Churches. In a book published in 1938, while he was president of the Federal Council of Churches, Jones wrote,

> It is a magnificent achievement to permeate a church with the spirit of reunion, to keep before every phase of congregational life the unanswered prayer of Jesus for the oneness of his followers, together with the inspiring stories of the apostles of unity, the men who caught this "vision splendid" and became flaming prophets of a reunited Christendom.[3]

As we hear this call to permeate the church with the spirit of Christian unity, we should recognize Jones's cultural context. At that time, the vast majority of church leaders were men. Today that is no longer true, as many apostles of unity are women. Additionally, the word "Christendom" has lost its savor. That is because the concept of Christendom is so deeply rooted in both institutionalism and even imperialism. So, it is being laid aside in service to Christ's mission. Nonetheless, even in this post-Christendom age, the prayer of unity that Jones mentions continues to have resonance.

> I pray they will be one, Father, just as you are in me and I am in you. I pray that they also will be in us, so that the world will believe that you sent me. I've given them the glory that you gave me so that they can be one just as we are one. I'm in them and you are in me so that they will be made perfectly one. Then the world will know that you sent me and that you have loved them just as you loved me. (John 17:21–23, CEB)

---

3. Jones, *This Great Business*, 89.

It is true that denominationalism isn't as fervent today as it was in the 1930s when Edgar DeWitt Jones ascended to the leadership of the ecumenical movement. Many of the nation's largest churches are at most loosely linked to a denomination if that. Indeed, many are denominations in themselves. While the institutional bonds have loosened, the Christian community continues to be deeply divided along ethnic, theological, cultural, economic, and political lines. Brand names may have lost value as seekers look for more generic forms, but many of the walls of division continue to stand in the way of true communion within the body of Christ.

It is possible to see the unifying presence of the Spirit at work within the Christian community. Much of this work occurs locally as congregations and individuals join together in interfaith groups, community organizing efforts, faith-based service opportunities, and community worship services, whether annual ones such as a Good Friday service, or occasional ones, like the ones that were held in many places across the country after the tragedy of September 11, 2001.

While cross-denominational ecumenical efforts are commendable, many of us live with the reality that division exists within our own faith traditions. One of the unfortunate realities of the history of the Stone-Campbell Movement is that they (we) compromised their witness because of internal divisions. There have been three major divisions within the movement, leading to the existence of the Churches of Christ, the Christian Churches/ Churches of Christ, and my own denomination, the Christian Church (Disciples of Christ). While these divisions are far from being healed, Jesus' vision of unity continues to call on those who participate in the broader faith community to pursue unity within the family even as they seek to build relationships with those outside the family. But it is important to note that not all unity is good unity. This is why it's not easy or convenient. It is easy to opt for safe unity, where in the pursuit of unity we fail to address matters of justice. It should be acknowledged that true unity, as José Morales observes, "is grounded in, and emerges from service and sacrifice. Between washing feet and taking up a cross." Thus, it is "dangerous and radical."[4]

With this reminder that the pursuit of true unity is "dangerous and radical," we turn to Psalm 133, which is one of my favorite passages of Scripture. It's only three verses long, but it captures the joy that comes from a family that is united. The first verse declares, "How very good and pleasant it is when kindred live together in unity!" The message is even clearer in the Common English Bible: "Look at how good and pleasing it is, when families live together as one!" Now, the family can be a rather small group. Families can become exclusive and focused on their own needs and agendas, and so looking back to José Morales's warning, this kind of unity would be safe, but possibly deadly. On the other hand, families can also be quite expansive, including people who don't share the same bloodline or even background. That's the point of verses 2 and 3. These verses expand our definition of family. To get a sense of how I receive this word from the psalmist, the paraphrase of the psalm by Michael Morgan might capture it best:

> How good when all the earth is one,
> And hearts embrace community;
> When strife will cease to separate,
> And love binds all in unity.[5]

It's quite possible that this psalm was written in the hope that the division between the northern and southern kingdoms of Israel and Judah would be healed. Mt. Hermon is, after all, in the northern region of Israel, and Zion or Jerusalem is at the center of the southern region. The references to the dew of Hermon and the precious oil that flows down the head and beard and robes of Aaron offer hope that movement can be made toward reuniting this divided family.

In this psalm, the focus is on Zion, which is where the temple stood. The psalmist holds out a vision of the people of God gathering in the city to experience the presence of God. Jerusalem often

---

4. Morales, "Heresy of Heresies," 45.

5. Morgan, *Psalter for Christian Worship*, 162.

stands as a symbol of God's presence. The prophets hold a vision of the nations gathering in Jerusalem to receive the blessings of God. We see this restated in the book of Revelation, where John offers a vision of the New Jerusalem descending from the heavens to the earth. The New Jerusalem is itself a sign that God is present with the people of God (Rev 21:1–8). You might say that Jerusalem is home to our family reunion. And regarding the makeup of this family, it's good to remember what Jesus said about his family. He told the crowd that his brothers and sisters and his mother were those who believed in him (Mark 3:35–36).

I wonder, might we extend this vision of unity beyond the bounds of the Christian faith? Over the last twenty-plus years, I have become deeply involved in interfaith work. One of the local interfaith organizations for which I have given leadership, the Troy-area Interfaith Group, takes this as its motto: "We believe that peace among peoples and nations requires peace among the religions." Getting to this place where religions are at peace with each other needn't involve looking for the lowest common denominator of agreement. Pluralism needn't require a relativism in which we all let go of our belief systems and practices. Over the years, I have discovered that interfaith conversations are best served when we respect the differences that exist between our religious traditions. While Judaism, Christianity, and Islam all trace our faith traditions back to Abraham (and beyond), that doesn't mean we look at things the same way.

I believe that Christians, Jews, and Muslims worship the same God. I believe this is an inheritance of our Abrahamic ancestry. Most Christians would assume that we worship the same God as the Jews, even if Christians envision God through a trinitarian lens. We don't always look at Islam in the same fashion, even though it too is a strict monotheistic faith that looks back to Abraham as its founder. Miroslav Volf notes three central beliefs shared in common between Muslims and Christians. Both affirm that there is only one God. Both affirm the premise that God has created everything that is not God. And finally, both affirm that God is different from what is not God. But, of course, there is more to this than three affirmations (this is the point of Volf's book *Allah*). The point is all three Abrahamic religions see themselves as believing in the God who called Abraham to be God's messenger.[6] When it comes to conversations with friends who are adherents of Dharmic religions such as Hinduism, Buddhism, and Sikhism, the differences are greater than those experienced among the Abrahamic religions. However, greater differences don't prevent us from having fruitful conversations or finding points of agreement, especially on matters of social justice and the integrity of creation. It has been recognized that something akin to the call to love one's neighbor is found in most religions. That seems to be a good starting place for not only achieving peace but moving toward the flourishing of creation. Any form of unity that exists across religious lines will be different from that pursued within the Christian family, but it is an important part of our calling (at least it is for me).

Unity begins in the family and then moves in concentric circles outward. Therefore, we can think of a congregation as a family. Paul uses the word *adelphos* (brother) some 127 times, and it is used 317 times in the whole of the New Testament. Also, the word *adelphē* (sister) is used twenty-six times in the New Testament and six times in Paul's letters. While *adelphē* is used in a gendered manner, *adelphos* is often used in a non-gendered way. Thus, the concept of "sibling" is even more prominent in Paul's letters for the Christian community than terms such as "body of Christ," "saints," or "church." Based on this evidence, Scot McKnight suggests that we would be well served to embrace the metaphor of "sibling" to describe our existence as members of the Christian community. When it comes to the responsibilities of pastors, McKnight suggests that Paul would have them "nurture a culture of siblings." He writes that "the apostle Paul constantly called his churches siblings, and the constant thinking of them as siblings and calling them siblings built a culture of siblingship rather than a culture of an audience, souls, students, or those in need of mediation."[7]

6. Volf, *Allah*, 97–98.

7. McKnight, *Pastor Paul*, 60–62.

This metaphor of being part of a family or siblingship brings to mind the theme song of the 1979 Pittsburgh Pirates during their World Series matchup against the Baltimore Orioles. The Pirates adopted as their theme song "We Are Family," a song from the group Sister Sledge. The message the song sent in this context was that all of Pittsburgh, and all the Pirates' fans across the nation, were part of one big family. That autumn, during the World Series of 1979, I numbered myself as one of the family, and I don't think the people of Pittsburgh minded! Now as the church family, we can be exclusive or inclusive. The choice is ours.

There are different ways in which we are family, including the church, but it's good to remember that we are ultimately part of the human family. As part of this family, we're called to unity for three reasons. We might start with the fact that this unity brings with it a sense of encouragement, as we learn from one another and find support from one another. We, hopefully, find this within our families, but also from others, especially from those whose traditions are different from our own. Additionally, it brings glory to God our Creator. That is, by loving one another we give glory to the God whom we are called to love with our entire being. This unity that we experience within the faith community and beyond enables us to be a blessing to the peoples of this earth. Indeed, by finding unity with one another, without uniformity, we can be a blessing to all of creation. And that is our covenant calling as children of Abraham and Sarah. Yes, we are one in Christ. "Somos Uno en Cristo!"

Reflection Questions for Individuals

1. What does the principle of unity in diversity mean to you?

2. Where have you seen or experienced unity in the Christian community? What forms did it take? Why might some forms be dangerous or destructive?

3. If unity within the Christian community is a blessing and a foundation for mission, how might unity be expressed beyond the boundaries of the Christian community? That is,

how might interreligious or interfaith engagement be an expression of unity in diversity that brings a blessing to the nations?

Reflection Questions for Congregations

1. Looking at its ministries and relationships, how does the congregation understand its place in the broader Christian community? How does it engage with congregations and churches outside its own tradition?

2. How does interfaith and interreligious engagement fit into the congregation's mission? How might this fit into a vision of unity in diversity?

3. How might the congregation's relationships and engagements, both ecumenical and interreligious, be an expression of the calling of Abraham and Sarah to be a blessing to the nations? What are some tangible ways in which this occurs?

8

What's in a Name?
—Discovering Spiritual DNA

"As for me, this is my covenant with you: You shall be the ancestor of a multitude of nations. No longer shall your name be Abram, but your name shall be Abraham; for I have made you the ancestor of a multitude of nations. I will make you exceedingly fruitful; and I will make nations of you, and kings shall come from you. I will establish my covenant between me and you, and your offspring after you throughout their generations, for an everlasting covenant, to be God to you and to your offspring after you." . . . God said to Abraham, "As for Sarai your wife, you shall not call her Sarai, but Sarah shall be her name. I will bless her, and moreover I will give you a son by her. I will bless her, and she shall give rise to nations; kings of peoples shall come from her." —GENESIS 17:4–7, 15–16

HOW DID YOU GET your name? As for me, I am named after my father, Robert David Cornwall Sr. My father was concerned about the family legacy, and so he chose to name me after himself. I chose differently. When our son was born, Cheryl and I looked at other names. The name we chose for him was taken from the roster of the San Francisco Giants. Brett, who was born in 1990, was named after the center fielder from the 1989 National League Champion San Francisco Giants. This was a compromise choice because Cheryl rejected my first choice—Will Clark Cornwall (Will was the Giants' all-star first baseman at the time). Unfortunately, Brett's namesake signed with the rival Dodgers the next year. Nevertheless, our son's name reflects our love of the Giants. The names our parents choose for us reflect the eras in which we were born, our family heritage, and even our cultural climate. Some names endure and others don't. Some come back in style from time to time just like paisley ties.

In the modern Western world, we don't usually think about the meanings of names. We choose them more for their aesthetics and perhaps to reflect family traditions. On the other hand, names often have meanings in the biblical story. In the Gospel of Matthew, the angel tells Joseph to name the couple's child Jesus, because he will save the people from their sins. Jacob's name gets changed to Israel, because "he has striven with God, and has prevailed" (Gen 32:28). Then there are names that Hosea gave to his children: "Not Pitied" and "Not My People" (Hos 1:2–9). Those names will never make it to the top of the "favorite baby names" list.

In Genesis 12, the guiding passage for our journey, we read of the call of Abram, and by extension, his spouse Sarai, to leave their families and travel to a strange land, with the promise that through their descendants the nations would be blessed. When we come to Genesis 17, we read a different version of the story. In this version of the call, God changes the names of Abram and Sarai to reflect a change in circumstances. By the time we get to Genesis 17, the family has arrived in Canaan. Their status changes from nomads to permanent residents. When God makes a covenant with Abram in Genesis 17, God declares, "I will make my covenant between me and you, and will make you exceedingly numerous." It is here that God changes Abram's name, even as God promises to give to Abram and his descendants the land in which they now dwell. "No longer shall your name be Abram, but your name shall be Abraham; for I have made you the ancestor of a multitude of nations. I will make you exceedingly fruitful; and I will make nations of you, and kings shall come from you. I will establish my covenant between me and you, and your offspring after you throughout their generations, for an everlasting covenant, to be God to you and to your offspring after you" (Gen 17:5–7). As a sign of the covenant, all males in the community are to be circumcised (Gen 17:10). Not only does God change Abram's name to Abraham, but God changes Sarai's name to Sarah because she will give birth to the heir of the covenant promise (Gen 17:15–22). This change reflects the changing circumstances they found themselves in, but perhaps we can hear a word of wisdom about our situation in these stories. Perhaps that word is this: God is present with us when we're on the road and when we're at home. In both situations, we are called to be a blessing.

Although I ended up going with a different title for the book, I started out titling this book "Reclaiming Founding Visions." I could have chosen as an alternative "Rediscovering our Spiritual DNA." Though I didn't choose to go with it either, in many ways this book is about spiritual DNA. After all, DNA is connected to one's family heritage. So, my question is this: How does our heritage influence our spiritual identity? Since I'm also asking congregations to wrestle with questions of identity, how does a congregation's name reflect its spiritual DNA?

The congregation I serve is known as Central Woodward Christian Church. It has carried that name since 1926 and it followed the congregation's move from Detroit to Troy in 1979. You could say that this church has a name with a history that doesn't fit the current location or ministry. But it survived the move from Detroit to the suburbs because it had meaning for members of the congregation. That move was over forty years in the past; the church will most likely change the name at some point in the future, but the name says something about the church and its purpose.

When names change, they may signal a change of circumstances or purposes. My alma mater, like many Christian colleges, has gone through the process of changing its name to reflect new realities. This decision hasn't sat well with many of my classmates who have fond memories of their student days. The changes produce a sense of grief. For those of us who lived under the former names of the school, questions have arisen as to whether the college remains rooted in its founding visions. The truth is, the school's academic focus has changed, which is why the name change has become necessary. Nevertheless, the school's core values remain rooted, as far as I can tell, in its founding vision.

When it comes to the church I serve in Michigan, the name has symbolic value to its members. Some elements are rooted in the past that may not completely reflect the present or future direction of the congregation, but they do speak of founding visions. I sense that this might true for many congregations. So, take the word "church." What does that word describe? Does it speak of a building or a community of people? Many congregations have chosen to forgo the word "church," thinking it reflects certain institutional values that it wants to eschew. Thus, the congregation I was a member of during high school, a Pentecostal congregation, used the term "Christian Center" rather than church. As time has passed, congregations have gotten even more creative in their attempts to name themselves, often hiding the fact that they are churches.

Nevertheless, the word "church" remains part of our vocabulary, and it reflects certain theological understandings. The Greek word we translate as church is *ekklesia*, which contextually speaks of an "assembly." Paul sometimes refers to the church as the "body of Christ." This suggests that it is a living, growing organism. Another word used by Paul is *adelphos*, or brother, which we might better translate as sibling, suggesting that the church is a family. This body/family may exist in a building, or it may not! In either case, it remains a church.

Then there is the word "Christian," which in our case has a denominational reference point. Hopefully, it also speaks of our connection to Jesus Christ. The same is true of the parenthetical identifier of "Disciples of Christ." Thus, our full name connects us with our denomination, the Christian Church (Disciples of Christ). Hopefully, that parenthetical identifier is more than a denominational moniker, so that in claiming this name we identify ourselves as followers of Christ. Of course, since we emphasize the freedom of the individual to determine what we believe, there will be diverse understandings of what it means to be a follower of Jesus.

So, what might the words "Central" and "Woodward" say about the congregation? They have geographical connotations, especially the word "Woodward." The combination of these two words serves as a reminder that this congregation is the fruit of a merger between two congregations that took place in 1926 (Central Christian Church and Woodward Avenue Christian Church). After the merger, these two congregations contributed equally to the identity of the church that would emerge. Central contributed its pastor, financial gifts, and distinguished leadership. Woodward Avenue contributed its property and a very active group of young families. What emerged was a congregation that was well situated to represent the Disciples of Christ in one of America's fastest-growing cities. Under the leadership of Edgar DeWitt Jones, this newly merged congregation grew in number and influence (this influence extended from Detroit outward to the rest of Michigan and then nationally, and even internationally, as the Detroit congregation was linked to congregations across the river in Windsor, Canada). Over the years the congregation has had its ups and downs so that by the 1970s it became clear that it could no longer sustain its neo-Gothic building in Detroit. So, it migrated north to our current location in Troy. Although the church no longer lived on Woodward Avenue, it kept the name. There have been discussions about changing the name, but the name has stuck with us (so far). The question is, what do these words that form our name say about our spiritual DNA?

If we were to change our name to reflect the changing circumstances, the easiest solution would be to drop the "Woodward" from our name. We haven't been located on Woodward Avenue (it lies about two miles west of us) for more than forty years. But, until we make that change, what might the "Woodward" part of our name signify? What spiritual DNA does "Woodward" contribute to our identity? There's heritage attached to the name, of course, but is that all?

As I've contemplated our name and engaged in conversations with members of the congregation, as well as with at least one former minister, I came to see in the name a connection between a suburban congregation and the community of origins. In fact, I felt that it helped solidify our commitment to ministries in Detroit over the years, ministries that have included work with Motown Mission, Gospel in Action Detroit, and Head Start of Detroit. Those ministries exist in the city of Detroit, but Woodward Avenue doesn't end at 8 Mile Road. It continues northward into Oakland County, moving north and west toward Pontiac. As such, Woodward Avenue is the spine that links the region. Our broader ministries link us to this spine, including a long-standing ministry partnership with the Congregational Church of Birmingham (United Church of Christ), which lies on the other side of Woodward Avenue. They are closer to Woodward than we are, but it serves as a good reminder of ministries that are connected to this road.

As for the word "Central," here are my thoughts. First of all, I think it might speak of our center, which is Jesus the Christ. Whatever we are as a congregation, we find our center in Jesus. It also speaks of a location, a home base. In Genesis 17, a nomadic people find a place to settle down and make a home. Or as we read it in the Common English Bible, God promised Abraham and his descendants "the land in which you are immigrants" (Gen 17:8, CEB). Having moved from our Detroit home on Woodward Avenue, we found a new home at the corner of Big Beaver and Adams in the city of Troy. We came to this place as immigrants, and we found a home here. Many of the congregants come from farther away than others to be present spiritually in the building that lies at the corner of Big Beaver and Adams.

If this place is our home, it is also the starting place for our ministries. If Genesis 12 gives us our purpose, which is to be a blessing to the nations, then Acts 1:8 gives us our game plan. Jesus told the disciples that they would receive power when the Holy

Spirit came upon them, and after receiving this empowerment, they were to take the good news to the ends of the earth, starting in Jerusalem (or in the case of my congregation, in the city of Troy) and then moving outward from there to the rest of Metro Detroit, Michigan, and beyond.

There is a vision statement that appears on the bulletin cover from Central Christian Church that dates to 1921. I'm not sure we'd put it the same way today, but I think it has meaning for us: "Central Church has a vision and a purpose of usefulness in Detroit far beyond its present location and equipment." At the time the congregation was expecting to build a new home, so that's part of the meaning of this statement, but I like the idea that they envisioned themselves as being useful to the community "far beyond its present location and equipment." Isn't that our calling, to be useful, or to be a blessing, to our community far beyond our current location?

In February 1922 Edgar DeWitt Jones faced a dilemma. The vision that had drawn him to Detroit seemed to be fading away. He wondered if he'd made a mistake coming to Detroit. In a letter to a friend, he spoke of his fondness for Central Christian Church, but he believed that the congregation faced a choice. It could go forward or it could go backward. So, he writes, "I think it has an extraordinary opportunity, but it simply cannot rest upon its oars. It must go forward or it will go back."[1] If it chose to go backward, then he knew he would have to move on. In the end, the congregation chose to go forward, and as time wore on, in part due to the merger with Woodward Avenue Christian Church, the vision that drew him to Detroit bore fruit. What was that vision? It centered on offering a progressive Christian voice that emphasized the Disciple commitment to the pursuit of Christian unity. In many ways, this is the founding vision of the congregation, the source of its original spiritual DNA.

When it comes to the life of a congregation, each of us contributes spiritual DNA to the body of Christ that is present in a

---

1. Edgar DeWitt Jones to Charles Dunscomb, February 6, 1922, Edgar DeWitt Jones Papers, Disciples of Christ Historical Society, Bethany, WV.

specific location. This is added to the spiritual DNA contributed by our spiritual ancestors in this congregation, including the vision of Edgar DeWitt Jones. That vision included openness to differing theological and political views, a commitment to the welfare of the community, a pursuit of Christian unity, and a commitment to world peace. Over time we followed this vision and identified ourselves as an open and affirming congregation, signaling our welcome of our LGBTQ brothers and sisters. This move might not have been on Jones's radar in the 1920s, but it fits the original vision.

Of course, there are other elements of our heritage that simply can't be reclaimed. They represent a different time and place. As we consider our heritage as a congregation we should keep in mind this word of wisdom provided to us by Dr. Jones himself: "If the church has become institutionalized, bereft of spiritual charm, and in bondage to outworn and discredited methods, the average man will pass it by and find his inspirations and comradeships elsewhere." But, as Dr. Jones noted, since the first century, when times have changed, the church has "adopted methods suitable to the time and the need."[2]

The calling remains present with us, signified by the change of names of Abraham and Sarah. They are our spiritual ancestors, passing on to us the covenant calling to be a blessing to the nations. Sarah still didn't have a child when the name change went into effect, but God made it clear that she would be the mother of nations. Yes, she laughed, but in the end, the promise was fulfilled.

Reflection Questions for Individuals

1. What is your name? What does it say about you?

2. Thinking about the story of Abraham and Sarah, and their name change, where do you sense God calling you? What are the signs of this calling?

---

2. Jones, *Blundering into Paradise*, 85–86.

3. If you are a part of a congregation, what does its name say to you? What are its identity and its mission?

Reflection Questions for Congregations

1. What is the full name of your congregation? What does each component of the name signify? How does it define its spiritual DNA?

2. Considering the congregational name just explored, how does it speak of the congregation's mission in the community and beyond? What is distinctive about the congregation's identity?

3. If you were to change the name of your congregation, what would that name change signify?

Epilogue

I am who I am, spiritually, because of the spiritual DNA I carry. My journey has been a circuitous one. I have traveled from the church of my birth, the Episcopal Church, to the Christian Church (Disciples of Christ), the church of my mature years. Along the way, I've been part of several other faith communities, including Pentecostals, Baptists, Presbyterians, and the Evangelical Covenant Church. My theology is eclectic. I've suggested this eclecticism is due to my being a historical theologian rather than a systematic one. My theology professor in seminary, Colin Brown, reinforced the idea that there is no one system of theology, which is why we didn't have a specific textbook. Over the years, I've borrowed from Karl Barth, Jürgen Moltmann, Dietrich Bonhoeffer, Jon Sobrino, Elizabeth Johnson, Athanasius, the Cappadocians, Augustine, John Calvin, Open Theists, and many more. I know that these can be strange bedfellows (think of Calvin and Augustine alongside Tom Oord), but I've come to believe that few of us are theological purists. Another way of describing my journey is to use the word "pilgrim." Diana Butler Bass writes that "becoming a pilgrim means becoming a local who adopts a new place and new identity by learning a new language and new rhythms and practices. Unlike the tourist, a pilgrim's goal is not to escape life, but to embrace it more deeply, to be transformed wholly as a person, with new ways of being in community and new hopes for the world."[1]

Over the years, I've spent time among those who value tradition and those who don't. Some communities are eager to reset

1. Bass and Stewart-Sicking, *From Nomads to Pilgrims*, xii.

things while others emphasize spiritual power and giftedness. I've been part of communities that emphasize mission and evangelism as well as social justice. I've experienced a vision of freedom and found a call to unity. In the course of my journey, I've also found myself deeply immersed in interfaith relationships, which I deeply value. Institutionally, my spiritual DNA includes Episcopal (tradition), Foursquare Gospel (restoration and spiritual power), evangelical (sharing the good news), and Disciples (freedom, unity, and restoration) elements. Time spent among the Baptists, the Presbyterians, and the Evangelical Covenant Church fit in there someplace as well. They are all elements of my spiritual journey, which continues to evolve, especially as I venture further into interfaith work. Along the way, I've had new experiences, but more importantly, the time spent locally has transformed me. I have become someone new.

While this book invites readers, both as individuals and as congregations, to explore their spiritual roots to discern the treasure and dross that has formed them, I expect that this process of looking back will enable the readers to envision the future, which they will help create. This isn't merely an exercise in nostalgia, though there might be a bit of nostalgia involved. It might also involve experiences of grief. Even when we grieve losses, we have, as Michael Girlinghouse suggests, the biblical story, including the stories of Abraham and his descendants, to guide us as we move into the future. He writes, "As we remember the stories of God's steadfast love and unwavering faithfulness, we are strengthened and encouraged by God's promise to walk with us through the valley of the shadow of death and to make all things new in Jesus Christ."[2] When we look back at our spiritual roots we will discover treasure and dross, but also those moments when we experienced God's faithfulness. This also engenders trust in God as we can take hold of an eschatological vision that speaks of hope. We are products of our past, but we are not limited by those experiences. That is because our spiritual journeys are not complete as long as we live.

2. Girlinghouse, *Embracing God's Future*, 253.

It is said by some that we should live in the present. That is true, but it's important to remember that the present only exists for a moment before it becomes the past. As for the future, it is always beckoning us forward. Jürgen Moltmann reminds us, "Original and true Christianity is a *movement of hope* in this world, which is often so arrogant and yet so despairing. That also makes it a *movement of healing* for sick souls and bodies. And not least, it is a *movement of liberation* for life, in opposition to the violence which oppresses the people."[3] Whatever spiritual DNA we draw from these founding visions, if it's true to the calling given to Abraham and his descendants, then it will be a vision of hope, healing, and liberation. Thus, it will be a call to bless.

What is true of us as individuals is also true for congregations. Congregations are formed by people who bring their various spiritual journeys and life experiences into the community. Some participants grow up in the church and others do not. Some spend their entire lives in one tradition, while others have been wanderers (much like Abraham, the wandering Aramean, who is the father of Israel). When we gather together as a community, or better yet, as siblings in the family of God, we contribute our diverse spiritual DNA into the church's existence. This contributes to the diversity and complexity of the congregation, even one steeped in a particular tradition. The members/participants in a congregation contribute their spiritual DNA, but so does the Tradition of which they are part.

So, for example, consider my denomination, the Christian Church (Disciples of Christ). Contributors to our identity as a movement and denomination include the Presbyterian heritage of the Disciples founders. It also includes the time spent by the Campbellites among the Baptists. They drew from the Reformation, along with the British Enlightenment (John Locke, for example). Then there is the secular DNA contributed by their American context. The movement emerged shortly after the birth of the new nation. Thomas Campbell contributed a founding document to the movement that he titled *The Declaration and Address*. The

3. Moltmann, *Sun of Righteousness, Arise!*, 115.

word "Declaration" was used purposely as a signal that this was a revolutionary document. Sometimes we Disciples see ourselves as part of the Reformed tradition, but if so, we are aren't an "orthodox" version of that tradition. The founders purposely threw off the creeds and faith statements prized by their Presbyterian colleagues and ancestors.

If we take this a step further, individual believers and the congregations of which they are members contribute their spiritual DNA to the larger church, making the Christian "religion" a rather complex organism. In our diversity and complexity, we find our purpose as a community in that call given to Abraham and Sarah. Their call is our founding vision, one that was embodied and renewed and passed on to us in Christ Jesus. That calling, which required them to leave their homes and set out for an unknown land, eventuated in a fountain of descendants, who are called to be a blessing to the nations. It is a calling that has been passed on from generation to generation until it incorporated we the readers of this book, whether Jew or gentile, for all of us are heirs of this call to be a blessing to humanity and all of creation. While the future might be open, might we envision that moment when all things come together, and the blessings promised to Abraham and Sarah reach their fulfillment?

> I did not see a temple in the city, because the Lord God Almighty and the Lamb are its temple. The city does not need the sun or the moon to shine on it, for the glory of God gives it light, and the Lamb is its lamp. The nations will walk by its light, and the kings of the earth will bring their splendor into it. On no day will its gates ever be shut, for there will be no night there. The glory and honor of the nations will be brought into it. (Rev 21:22–26, NIV)

Bibliography

Augustine. *Confessions.* Translated with Introduction by Henry Chadwick. Oxford: Oxford University Press, 1991. Kindle Edition.

—————. *On Christian Doctrine.* Edited by Philip Schaff. Translated by Marcus Dods and J. F. Shaw. Aeterna, 2011. Kindle Edition.

Bass, Diana Butler. *A People's History of Christianity: The Other Side of the Story.* San Francisco: HarperOne, 2009.

Bass, Diana Butler, and Joseph Stewart-Sicking, eds. *From Nomads to Pilgrims: Stories from Practicing Congregations.* Herndon, VA: Alban Institute, 2006.

Bendroth, Margaret. *The Spiritual Practice of Remembering.* Grand Rapids: Eerdmans, 2013.

Blue, Debbie. *Consider the Women: A Provocative Guide to Three Matriarchs of the Bible.* Grand Rapids: Eerdmans, 2019.

Boring, M. Eugene, and Fred B. Craddock. *The People's New Testament Commentary.* Louisville: Westminster John Knox, 2009.

Brett, Thomas. *Tradition Necessary to Explain and Interpret the Holy Scriptures.* 1718.

Campbell, Alexander. *The Christian System.* Reprint. Salem, NH: Ayer, 1988.

Campbell, Thomas. "Declaration and Address." In *The Quest for Christian Unity, Peace and Purity in Thomas Campbell's Declaration and Address,* edited by Thomas H. Olbricht and Hans Rollmann, 3–58. Lanham, MD: Scarecrow, 2000.

Chilcote, Paul Wesley. *Recapturing the Wesleys' Vision: An Introduction to the Faith of John and Charles Wesley.* Downers Grove: IVP Academic, 2009.

Cornwall, Robert D. *The Authority of Scripture in a Postmodern Age: Some Help from Karl Barth.* Topical Line Drives 9. Gonzalez, FL: Energion, 2014.

—————. *The Eucharist: Encounters with Jesus at the Table.* Topical Line Drives 10. Gonzalez, FL: Energion, 2014.

—————. *Freedom in Covenant: Reflections on the Distinctive Values and Practices of the Christian Church (Disciples of Christ).* Eugene, OR: Wipf and Stock, 2015.

—————. "Primitivism and the Redefinition of Dispensationalism in the Theology of Aimee Semple McPherson." *Pneuma* 14.1 (1992) 23–42.

———. *Unfettered Spirit: Spiritual Gifts for the New Great Awakening.* Gonzalez, FL: Energion, 2013.

———. *Visible and Apostolic: The Constitution of the Church in High Church and Non-Juror Thought.* Newark, DE: University of Delaware Press, 1993.

Crouch, Andy. *Playing God: Redeeming the Gift of Power.* Downers Grove: InterVarsity, 2013.

Cunningham, Frank J. *Vesper Time: The Spiritual Practice of Growing Older.* Maryknoll, NY: Orbis, 2019.

Duck, Ruth. *Worship for the Whole People of God: Vital Worship for the 21st Century.* Louisville: Westminster John Knox, 2013.

Duerksen, Darren T., and William A. Dyrness. *Seeking Church: Emerging Witnesses to the Kingdom.* Downers Grove: IVP Academic, 2019.

Espinoza, Gaston. "Ordinary Prophet: William J. Seymour and the Azusa Street Revival." In *The Azusa Street Revival and Its Legacy*, edited by Harold D. Hunter and Cecil M. Robeck Jr., 29–60. Eugene, OR: Wipf and Stock, 2009.

Feiler, Bruce. *Abraham: A Journey to the Heart of Three Faiths.* New York: William Morrow, 2002.

Girlinghouse, Michael K. *Embracing God's Future without Forgetting the Past: A Conversation about Loss, Grief, and Nostalgia in Congregational Life.* Minneapolis: Fortress, 2019.

González, Justo L. *The Mestizo Augustine: A Theologian between Two Cultures.* Downers Grove: IVP Academic, 2016.

Gossai, Hemchand. *Barrenness and Blessing: Abraham, Sarah, and the Journey of Faith.* Eugene, OR: Cascade, 2008.

Guarino, Thomas G. *Vincent of Lérins and the Development of Christian Doctrine.* Grand Rapids: Baker Academic, 2013.

Gushee, David P. *Still Christian: Following Jesus out of American Evangelicalism.* Louisville: Westminster John Knox, 2017.

Gushee, David P., and Colin Holtz. *Moral Leadership for a Divided Age: Fourteen People Who Dared to Change Our World.* Grand Rapids: Brazos, 2018.

Hays, Richard B. "The Letter to the Galatians: Introduction, Commentary, and Reflections." In *The New Interpreter's Bible*, edited by Leander Keck, 11:181–347. Nashville: Abingdon, 2000.

Holbert, John. "The Lynchpin of the Bible: Reflections on Genesis 12:1–4a." *Patheos*, March 14, 2011. https://www.patheos.com/resources/additional-resources/2011/03/lynchpin-of-the-bible-john-holbert-03-14-2011.

Janzen, J. Gerald. *Abraham and All the Families of the Earth: A Commentary on Genesis 12–50.* International Theological Commentary. Grand Rapids: Eerdmans, 1993.

Jones, Edgar Dewitt. *Blundering into Paradise.* Harper & Brothers, 1932.

———. *Sermons I Love to Preach.* New York: Harper & Brothers, 1953.

———. *This Great Business of Being a Christian.* New York: Harper & Brothers, 1938.

Kim, Grace Ji-Sun. *Reimagining Spirit: Wind, Breath, and Vibration.* Eugene, OR: Cascade, 2019.

Kim, Grace Ji-Sun, and Susan M. Shaw. *Intersectional Theology: An Introductory Guide*. Minneapolis: Fortress, 2018.

Mattson, Ingrid. "How to Read the Quran." In *The Study Quran: A New Translation and Commentary*, edited by Seyyed Hossein Nasr, 1587–1600. San Francisco: HarperOne, 2015.

McKnight, Scot. *Pastor Paul: Nurturing a Culture of Christoformity in the Church*. Grand Rapids: Brazos, 2019.

McPherson, Aimee Semple. *The Foursquare Gospel*. Compiled by Raymond L. Cox. Los Angeles: Foursquare, 1969.

Moltmann, Jürgen. *Sun of Righteousness, Arise! God's Future for Humanity and the Earth*. Translated by Margaret Kohl. Minneapolis: Fortress, 2010.

Morgan, Michael. *The Psalter for Christian Worship*. Revised ed. Louisville: Westminster John Knox, 2019.

Morales, José F., Jr. "Heresy of Heresies: 'From Deadly Unity to Life-Giving Unity.'" In *Preaching as Resistance: Voices of Hope, Justice, & Solidarity*, edited by Phil Snider, 41–47. St. Louis: Chalice, 2018,

Oord, Thomas Jay. *God Can't: How to Believe in God and Love after Tragedy, Abuse, and Other Evils*. Nampa, ID: SacraSage, 2019.

———. *The Uncontrolling Love of God: An Open and Relational Account of Providence*. Downers Grove: IVP Academic, 2015.

Osborn, Ronald. *Experiment in Liberty: The Ideal of Freedom in the Experience of the Disciples of Christ*. St. Louis: Bethany, 1978.

Pelikan, Jaroslav. *The Vindication of Tradition: The 1983 Jefferson Lectures*. New Haven: Yale University Press, 1984.

Reese, Martha Grace. *Unbinding the Gospel: Real Life Evangelism*. 2nd edition. St. Louis: Chalice, 2008.

———. *Unbinding Your Heart: 40 Days of Prayer and Faith Sharing*. St. Louis: Chalice, 2008.

Rohr, Richard. *Things Hidden: Scripture as Spirituality*. Cincinnati: St. Anthony Messenger, 2007.

Schwartz, Barry L. *Path of the Prophets: The Ethics-Driven Life*. Philadelphia: Jewish Publication Society, 2018.

Stanglin, Keith. *The Letter and Spirit of Biblical Interpretation: From the Early Church to Modern Practice*. Grand Rapids: Baker Academic, 2018.

Vincent of Lérins. *Commonitory*. Translated by C. A. Heurtley. In Nicene and Post-Nicene Fathers Second Series, edited by Philip Schaff and Henry Wace, 11. Buffalo, NY: Christian Literature, 1894. Revised and edited for New Advent by Kevin Knight. http://www.newadvent.org/fathers/3506.htm.

Volf, Miroslav. *Allah: A Christian Response*. San Francisco: HarperOne, 2011.

———. *Flourishing: Why We Need Religion in a Globalized World*. New Haven: Yale University Press, 2015.

Watkins, Sharon. *Whole: A Call to Unity in our Fragmented World*. St. Louis: Chalice, 2014.

Williamson, Clark M. *Way of Blessing, Way of Life: A Christian Theology.* St. Louis: Chalice, 1999.

Yong, Amos. *Discerning the Spirit(s): A Pentecostal-Charismatic Contribution to Christian Theology of Religions.* Eugene, OR: Wipf and Stock, 2018.

———. *The Spirit Poured Out on All Flesh: Pentecostalism and the Possibility of Global Theology.* Grand Rapids: Baker Academic, 2005.

Lightning Source UK Ltd.
Milton Keynes UK
UKHW012032100122
396910UK00004B/1119